Hamlyn Kitchen Shelf

BARBECUES
AND GRILLS

Annette Wolter

Hamlyn
London · New York · Sydney · Toronto

Cover photograph by Paul Williams

This edition published by
The Hamlyn Publishing Group Limited
London · New York · Sydney · Toronto
Astronaut House, Feltham, Middlesex, England
© Copyright The Hamlyn Publishing Group Limited 1983

ISBN 0 600 32341 2

First published under the title
Grill-Vergnügen International
© Copyright by Gräfe und Unzer Verlag, München

Set in 10 on 11pt Monophoto Sabon 669
by Tameside Filmsetting Ltd,
Ashton-under-Lyne, Lancashire

Printed in Italy

Contents

Useful facts and figures

Notes on metrication

In this book quantities are given in metric and Imperial measures. Exact conversion from Imperial to metric measures does not usually give very convenient working quantities and so the metric measures have been rounded off into units of 25 grams. The table below shows the recommended equivalents.

Ounces	Approx g to nearest whole figure	Recommended conversion to nearest unit of 25
1	28	25
2	57	50
3	85	75
4	113	100
5	142	150
6	170	175
7	198	200
8	227	225
9	255	250
10	283	275
11	312	300
12	340	350
13	368	375
14	396	400
15	425	425
16 (1 lb)	454	450
17	482	475
18	510	500
19	539	550
20 ($1\frac{1}{4}$ lb)	567	575

Note: When converting quantities over 20 oz first add the appropriate figures in the centre column, then adjust to the nearest unit of 25. As a general guide, 1 kg (1000 g) equals 2.2 lb or about 2 lb 3 oz. This method of conversion give good results in nearly all cases, although in certain pastry and cake recipes a more accurate conversion is necessary to produce a balanced recipe.

Liquid measures The millilitre has been used in this book and the following table gives a few examples.

Imperial	Approx ml to nearest whole figure	Recommended ml
$\frac{1}{4}$ pint	142	150 ml
$\frac{1}{2}$ pint	283	300 ml
$\frac{3}{4}$ pint	425	450 ml
1 pint	567	600 ml
$1\frac{1}{2}$ pint	851	900 ml
$1\frac{3}{4}$ pints	992	1000 ml (1 litre)

Spoon measures All spoon measures given in this book are level unless otherwise stated.

Can sizes At present, cans are marked with the exact (usually to the nearest whole number) metric equivalent of the Imperial weight of the contents, so we have followed this practice when giving can sizes.

Oven temperatures

The table below gives recommended equivalents.

	°C	°F	Gas Mark
Very cool	110	225	$\frac{1}{4}$
	120	250	$\frac{1}{2}$
Cool	140	275	1
	150	300	2
Moderate	160	325	3
	180	350	4
Moderately hot	190	375	5
	200	400	6
Hot	220	425	7
	230	450	8
Very hot	240	475	9

Note: WHEN MAKING ANY OF THE RECIPES IN THIS BOOK, ONLY FOLLOW ONE SET OF MEASURES AS THEY ARE NOT INTERCHANGEABLE.

Introduction

Barbecuing has long been one of the most popular ways of cooking. The tempting, aromatic smell of food sizzling over hot coals, the exhileration of eating in the open air and – if you use disposable plates and cutlery – the added bonus of little washing up to do – these are all part of the joys of barbecuing.

Whether you are planning an open-air party on a summer evening or simply giving your family the fun of eating out of doors, you should find plenty of ideas here for all kinds of barbecues and grills. Traditional favourites like hamburgers and garlic bread have, of course, not been forgotten, but there is also a wide range of fish, meat, poultry and vegetable dishes, side salads, snacks and kebabs and even a section on grilled desserts. Cooking methods are no more difficult than for an ordinary electric or gas grill; in fact, if the weather or your mood is not conducive to barbecuing you need not lose out, as most of these recipes can be cooked equally as well under the grill. You may find, however, that some foods cook slightly faster.

While cooking methods may not differ greatly from grilling, the preparation of the barbecue itself does, of course, take a certain amount of knowledge and care. Here are some basic guidelines before you start.

Setting up your Barbecue

A barbecue is simply a grill positioned over a bed of hot coals. You can buy various types of portable charcoal-burning barbecues or, if you think you will be barbecuing a good deal, you can build your own.

Portable charcoal-burning barbecues These range from the hibachi, a small barbecue originally from Japan which comes either in table-top form or free-standing, to the larger, open barbecue or brazier, which can cope with greater quantities than the hibachi. The more sophisticated kinds of braziers have hoods which partially or even wholly cover the fire-bowl, thereby protecting the food and enabling it to cook more quickly.

Home-made and permanent barbecues You can construct an instant barbecue very simply by placing a grill pan rack on top of a large clay flower pot. Or you can build a permanent one from bricks and an iron grill, making sure that you site it a safe distance from the house.

Whatever kind of barbecue you opt for, make sure that it is strong and well-constructed and that the legs, if any, are stable and capable of bearing a fully laden grill. Check also that the grill can be positioned at a variety of distances from the coals. Most of the larger barbecues include a battery-operated rôtisserie which you will need if you want to cook large pieces of meat and this should consist of a strong steel spit with prongs attached at either end to hold the meat firmly in place.

Lighting the Fire

The usual fuel to use for portable barbecues is charcoal, either in lumpwood or briquette form. Charcoal briquettes are perhaps the more efficient of the two as they burn slowly and give off a good heat.

Both charcoal and wood can be burnt in home-made and permanent barbecues, the best wood being the hard, slow-burning kinds such as beech, oak and ash.

To prepare a charcoal-burning barbecue, line the fire-bowl with a sheet of cooking foil; this will both quicken cooking time by reflecting heat on to the food and make cleaning up easier. Spread a thin layer of gravel or sand on the base of the bowl and top this with enough charcoal briquettes or lumpwood charcoal to cover the base to a depth of 5–7.5 cm/2–3 in. Light the fire using matches, firelighters or a liquid fire starter (but follow the manufacturer's instructions carefully when doing this and always use a long taper to light the fire). Never use paraffin, petrol or kerosene; not only are they dangerous, they also spoil the taste of the food. After lighting, a charcoal fire should be ready for cooking in 30–40 minutes.

If you are burning wood, arrange the pieces in a well-ventilated pile, interspersed with kindling such as paper, shavings or soft wood sticks. Gradually add larger pieces of hard wood until you have a good fire. It should be ready for grilling after about 30 minutes; by this time the flames should have burnt out and covered the wood with a layer of white ash.

Cooking Equipment

Once you have your basic barbecue, all you need is a few extra items of equipment which will make life much easier for you.

Work surface You will need a firm table of a comfortable height, large enough to hold your cooking implements and still leave space to work on.

Tongs Preferably light and of a non-conductive material, these are very useful for turning food.

Gloves Oven gloves or other heat-proof gloves will protect your hands when dealing with the fire or handling hot food.

Spoons Use long spoons with heat-resistant handles to baste grilled foods.

Pastry brush You will need this to brush some foods lightly with oil, sauces or marinades while cooking.

Kebab skewers Allow one long or two short ones per person. Again, these should preferably have heat-resistant handles.

Meat thermometer Not absolutely necessary but a useful aid in telling you when large spit-roast joints of meat are cooked.

Cooking foil As well as making a heat-reflective lining for the fire-bowl, sheets of cooking foil can be placed between the food and the grill to prevent delicate foods from cooking too quickly, or wrapped around vegetables such as potatoes and aubergines which are then cooked directly on the hot coals.

Barbecuing Techniques

About 15 minutes before you start to cook, place the grill over the coals. Knock any ash off the wood or charcoal. Arrange the food on the grill and position the grill at the right height, according to whether the food requires hot, medium or low coals. For hot coals, the grill should be 5–7.5 cm/2–3 in above the fire. For a medium heat, raise it to about 10 cm/4 in above and for a low heat, raise it still higher. These distances of course will vary depending on how hot the fire becomes during cooking, so watch your barbecue carefully and adjust the height of the grill when it seems necessary.

Larger joints of meat will need to be cooked on the rôtisserie. When spit-roasting it is very important that the meat should not only sit securely on the spit, but that it should also be properly balanced. Skewer the meat as nearly along the middle of the joint as you can and rotate the spit in the palms of your hands to check that it is balanced. It should rotate at an even pace, not in fits and starts.

When you have finished barbecuing, snuff out the coals by transferring them to a metal bucket with a lid and store them for use another time.

Toasted tuna sandwiches

1 (198-g/7-oz can tuna in oil
1 dessert apple
1 onion
1 gherkin
1 red pepper
1 banana
½ teaspoon lemon juice
2 tablespoons chopped fresh parsley
pinch each of salt, pepper and sugar
12 slices white bread
40 g/1½ oz butter or margarine

Drain the tuna, keeping the oil on one side. Peel, core and grate the apple. Finely dice the onion. Drain and finely dice the gherkin. Halve the red pepper, remove the seeds and pith, cut it into strips and then into small cubes. Crush the banana with a fork and mix it immediately with the grated apple and lemon juice. Break the tuna into small pieces and mix it with the apple, banana, onion, gherkin, red pepper, parsley, salt, pepper and sugar.

Spread the bread with the butter or margarine and cover six slices with the tuna mixture. Sandwich together with the remaining bread.

Grease six pieces of cooking foil with the tuna oil, wrap them round the sandwiches and cook the sandwiches on the barbecue or under the grill for 5 minutes on each side.

Carefully remove the sandwiches from the foil and cook them for a further minute on each side, until lightly toasted. **Serves 6**

Serve with: A plain tomato salad or a green salad.

Spanish onion slices

2 large red Spanish onions
about 50 g/2 oz butter or margarine
1 French loaf
1 (200-g/7.05-oz) packet cheese slices
pinch of paprika per slice of bread

Cut the onions into rings. Melt 20 g/¾ oz of the fat in a pan and fry the onions until transparent, turning them occasionally.

Cut the French bread into eight diagonal slices and spread these with the remaining butter or margarine. Halve the slices of cheese diagonally and place two triangles of cheese on each slice of bread. Top with a few onion rings, sprinkle with paprika and grill the slices under a hot grill until the cheese begins to melt. **Serves 4**

Serve with: Tomato salad or Mediterranean mixed salad (page 71).

Spanish onion slices.

Cheese and tomato rarebit

4 firm tomatoes
4 slices white bread
25 g/1 oz butter or margarine
salt and pepper to taste
4 slices Cheddar or Emmental cheese
generous pinch of dried oregano per portion

Cut the tomatoes into fairly thick slices. Toast one side of the bread and spread the untoasted sides with butter or margarine. Arrange the sliced tomato on top and season with salt and pepper. Top each portion with a slice of cheese, sprinkle it with oregano and cook it under the grill until the cheese begins to melt. **Serves 4**

Serve with: Green salad or Neapolitan salad (page 75).

Bacon and eggs in foil

2 tablespoons oil
4 eggs
$\frac{1}{2}$ teaspoon salt
generous pinch of pepper per egg
4 rashers streaky bacon
4 teaspoons tomato ketchup

Either use four aluminium foil plates or wrap pieces of cooking foil around four flame-proof dishes.

Divide the oil between the dishes and heat them on the barbecue. Tip one egg into each dish, season the egg white with salt and pepper and allow the egg to fry in the oil. Cook the bacon directly on the barbecue until brown and crisp. Serve the bacon with the eggs and garnish each portion with a teaspoon of tomato ketchup. **Serves 4**

Cheese and tomato rarebit.

Stuffed meat loaf

575 g/1¼ lb meat loaf or pork haslet, unsliced
1 dessert apple
½ teaspoon lemon juice
75 g/3 oz canned pimientoes
100 g/4 oz canned mushrooms
½ teaspoon mustard
pinch each of salt and sugar
1 teaspoon chopped fresh parsley
8 stuffed olives to garnish

Cut the meat loaf into four equal slices. Peel, quarter, core and grate the apple. Sprinkle the grated apple with the lemon juice. Drain and finely dice the pimientoes. Drain and slice the mushrooms. Mix the apple with the pimiento, mustard, mushrooms, salt, sugar and parsley.

Spread the filling over one half of each sausage slice and fold the other half over the top. Wrap each portion in cooking foil and cook the four parcels at a gentle heat on the barbecue or under the grill for 10 minutes, turning frequently. Serve garnished with olives and secured with cocktail sticks. **Serves 4**

Serve with: Brown bread, Charcoal-baked potatoes (page 62) and a green salad.

Portuguese sandwiches

8 slices white bread
butter or margarine for spreading
1 (113-g/4-oz) can sardines in oil
1 dessert apple
1 onion
3 tablespoons mayonnaise
½ teaspoon lemon juice
pinch of mustard powder
pinch each of pepper and dried basil
4 tomatoes, sliced
¼ teaspoon salt

Spread the bread with the butter or margarine. Drain and mash the sardines. Peel, core and grate the apple. Finely dice the onion.

Mix the sardines, apple and onion with the mayonnaise, lemon juice, mustard, pepper and basil to a smooth consistency and spread this on four of the slices of bread. Arrange the sliced tomatoes over the filling and sprinkle them with salt. Top with the remaining bread slices and wrap each sandwich in cooking foil. Cook them on the barbecue or under the grill for 5 minutes on each side, then carefully remove the foil and cook the sandwiches briefly until toasted on each side. **Serves 4**

Serve with: Creamy cucumber salad (page 76).

Fish finger burger

(Illustrated on pages 12–13)

50 g/2 oz butter
juice of 1 lemon
12 frozen fish fingers
6 bread rolls
2 onions
1 teaspoon paprika
1 teaspoon paprika
2 tablespoons oil

Melt the butter and stir in the lemon juice. Brush the fish fingers with the lemon butter and cook them on both sides over medium coals or under the grill, following the instructions on the packet.

Halve the rolls and lightly toast the cut surfaces on the barbecue or under the grill. Cut the onions into rings. Stir the paprika into the oil, dip the onion rings into the mixture and cook them lightly on both sides on the edge of the barbecue or under the grill.

Place two fish fingers on each of six of the half rolls, garnish generously with onion rings, top with the remaining half rolls and serve. **Serves 6**

Overleaf (left) Swiss sausage ring (page 18), served with a mixed salad; (right, from the top) Hungarian paprika chops (page 48), Fish finger burger (page 11), Rump steak with garlic and herb butter (page 42).

Grilled asparagus on toast

4 slices white bread
3 tomatoes
4 tablespoons mayonnaise
1 (283-g/10-oz) can asparagus tips
225 g/8 oz smoked or boiled ham
4 tablespoons grated mild Cheddar cheese
50 g/2 oz butter, cut into flakes

Lightly toast the bread on one side only. Slice the tomatoes. Spread the mayonnaise on the untoasted sides and top with the sliced tomatoes. Drain the asparagus tips and arrange them on the toast. Cut the ham into strips and lay them over the asparagus.

Sprinkle grated cheese over the top, followed by the flakes of butter. Cook the toasts under a hot grill for a few minutes, until the cheese begins to brown. **Serves 4**

Stuffed liver sausage rolls

4 rye or wholemeal rolls
1 small onion
1 egg yolk
pinch each of salt, pepper and dried marjoram
400 g/14 oz liver sausage
2 tablespoons dried breadcrumbs
25 g/1 oz butter, cut into flakes

Halve the rolls and remove the insides. Finely dice the onion. Work the egg yolk, onion, salt, pepper and marjoram into the liver sausage. Fill the eight eight half rolls with the liver sausage mixture, sprinkle breadcrumbs over the top and dot with butter. Grill the rolls under a hot grill for 5 minutes. **Serves 4**

Meatballs with ginger

225 g/8 oz minced pork or lamb
100 g/4 oz minced lean beef
1 egg, beaten
2 tablespoons fresh breadcrumbs
grated rind and juice of $\frac{1}{2}$ lemon
2 teaspoons curry powder
pinch each of salt and pepper
1 (1-cm/$\frac{1}{2}$-in) piece fresh root ginger
3 tablespoons oil

Mix the minced meats, beaten egg, breadcrumbs, lemon rind and juice, curry powder, salt and pepper together to a smooth consistency. Grate the ginger and stir it into the mixture.

With wet hands shape the mixture into balls about the size of a table-tennis ball and roll these in the oil. Thread the meatballs on to kebab skewers and cook them on the barbecue or under the grill at a moderate heat, turning frequently, for about 15 minutes, until they are thoroughly cooked. **Serves 4**

Serve with: Mandarin or pineapple segments and white bread.

Grilled asparagus on toast.

Russian meatballs

1 onion
40 g / 1½ oz butter
450 g / 1 lb minced beef or lamb
½ teaspoon salt
pinch each of pepper and grated nutmeg
1 egg, beaten
150 ml / ¼ pint soured cream

Finely dice the onion. Melt the butter in a small pan. Mix the minced meat to a smooth consistency with 1 tablespoon melted butter, 1 tablespoon diced onion, the salt, pepper, nutmeg and egg. Fry the remaining onion in the rest of the butter.

With moist hands shape the mixture into small meatballs and cook them at a moderate heat on the barbecue or under the grill for 10 minutes, turning once, until they are cooked on both sides.

Stir the fried onions into the soured cream and serve the sauce with the meatballs. **Serves 4**

Serve with: Potato salad or mashed potatoes.

Spicy beef sausages

450 g / 1 lb minced beef
bunch of parsley
1 clove garlic
40 g / 1½ oz butter
2 tablespoons flour
½ teaspoon salt
¼ teaspoon black pepper
¼ teaspoon paprika
2 tablespoons oil
4 onions

Place the minced beef in a large bowl. Finely chop the parsley. Peel and crush the garlic clove. Melt the butter in a small pan. Add the parsley, garlic, melted butter, flour, salt, pepper and paprika to the meat and work all the ingredients together to give a smooth mixture.

With wet hands shape the mixture into thick sausages about 5 cm / 2 in long. Brush these with oil and cook them under a hot grill or over hot coals for about 6 minutes, turning frequently and brushing them repeatedly with oil.

Finely chop the onions and serve them with the cooked sausages.

Serve with: French bread and a green salad.

Stuffed pepper rolls

1 bread roll
½ onion
4 small red peppers
350 g / 12 oz minced beef, pork or lamb
½ teaspoon salt
generous pinch of pepper
8 rashers streaky bacon
½ teaspoon paprika

Soften the bread roll in a little lukewarm water. Finely dice the onion. Halve the peppers lengthways and remove the seeds and pith.

Squeeze out the roll and mix it with the onion, minced meat, salt and pepper. Shape the mixture into eight rolls, each about the length of your finger, and put each roll inside half a pepper. Remove the rind from the bacon, sprinkle the rashers with paprika and wrap them around the stuffed peppers, securing them with small skewers or string. Cook the pepper rolls at a moderate heat on the barbecue or under the grill for 30 minutes, turning them repeatedly, until cooked through. **Serves 4**

Stuffed pepper rolls.

Hawaii kebabs

50 g/2 oz fresh breadcrumbs
350 g/12 oz minced beef
1 egg, beaten
juice of 1 lemon
½ teaspoon salt
generous pinch of pepper
2 tablespoons oil
2 canned peach halves
1 canned pineapple ring
100 g/4 oz Cheddar cheese
2 tablespoons fine dried breadcrumbs
1 teaspoon paprika
8 cocktail cherries

Mix the fresh breadcrumbs in a bowl with the mince, half the beaten egg, the lemon juice, salt and pepper. Shape the mixture into small, walnut-sized balls, heat half the oil in a frying pan and fry the meatballs over a low heat for a few minutes, turning them from time to time.

Drain the peach halves and pineapple ring and chop them into pieces about the same size as the meatballs. Cut the cheese also into walnut-sized cubes and dip these first into the remaining beaten egg, then into the dried breadcrumbs to coat thoroughly. Leave the cubes on one side.

Stir the paprika into the remaining oil. Arrange the meatballs, chopped fruit and cocktail cherries alternately on kebab skewers and cook the kebabs at a medium heat under the grill or on the barbecue for 4–5 minutes, turning frequently and brushing them several times with the paprika oil. Now thread the cheese cubes on to the skewers and cook for a further 2 minutes, until the cheese is just beginning to melt. **Serves 4**

Ham and cheese kebabs

350 g/12 oz Emmental cheese, unsliced
350 g/12 oz ham, unsliced
2 tomatoes
¼ teaspoon salt
100 g/4 oz canned mandarin segments
1 tablespoon oil

Remove the rind from the cheese and cut the cheese into bite-sized cubes, together with the

ham. Cut each tomato into eight wedges and season them with salt. Drain the mandarin segments, reserving 1 tablespoon of the juice.

Arrange the cheese, ham, tomatoes and mandarins alternately on kebab skewers. Stir the mandarin syrup into the oil and brush the kebabs with the mixture. Cook them under the grill or on the barbecue until the cheese begins to melt, turning frequently and brushing repeatedly with the oil. **Serves 4**

Serve with: Toasted white bread and butter.

Simple sausage kebabs

8 Frankfurter sausages
225 g/8 oz Cheddar cheese, sliced
150 g/5 oz thin bacon rashers
4–6 tomatoes
2 medium pickled cucumbers

Cut the sausages widthways into pieces about 5 cm/2 in long. Trim the cheese slices to the same length. Slice along the length of each piece of sausage to halfway through and fill the slits with a slice of cheese folded double. Remove the rind from the bacon and wrap each piece of sausage in a rasher. Quarter the tomatoes. Drain the pickled cucumbers, quarter them lengthways and cut the quarters into pieces.

Thread the stuffed sausages on kebab skewers, alternating them with tomato quarters and pieces of cucumber, and cook them for 15 minutes at a moderate heat under the grill or on the barbecue, turning frequently. **Serves 4**

Country-style mushroom kebabs

450 g / 1 lb large flat mushrooms
225 g / 8 oz button mushrooms
2 tomatoes
2 small onions
1 red pepper
150 g / 5 oz thick rashers streaky bacon
40 g / 1½ oz butter or margarine
generous pinch each of salt and pepper

Clean, trim and thickly slice all the mushrooms. Cut the tomatoes into eight wedges each. Thickly slice the onions. Halve the pepper, remove the seeds and pith and cut the flesh into chunks. Remove the rind from the bacon and cut the rashers into large pieces. Arrange pieces of mushroom, tomato, onion, pepper and bacon alternately on kebab skewers. Melt the butter or margarine, season it with the salt and pepper and brush the kebabs with the mixture. Cook them for 10 minutes under the grill or over fairly cool coals, turning frequently and brushing them repeatedly with melted fat. **Serves 4**

Gouda kebabs

225 g / 8 oz Bierwurst or ham sausage, unsliced
225 g / 8 oz cervelat sausage, unsliced
225 g / 8 oz matured Gouda cheese
2 bananas
2 pickled cucumbers
2 tablespoons beer

Remove the skin from the sausages and the rind from the Gouda and coarsely dice the meat and cheese. Cut the bananas into thick slices. Drain the pickled cucumbers and slice them thickly too.

Thread the pieces of cheese and sausage, banana and cucumber alternately on to four or more skewers and cook the kebabs at a moderate heat on the barbecue or under the grill for 8–10 minutes, turning frequently. During cooking brush the kebabs frequently with beer.

Serve with: Garlic Bread (page 64)

Country-style mushroom kebabs.

Curried sausage ring

50 g/2 oz Emmental or Cheddar cheese
1 onion
1 green pepper
1 pickled cucumber
100 g/4 oz streaky bacon
1 (454-g/1-lb) or 2 (227-g/8-oz) smoked Dutch
sausages
oil for grilling
½ teaspoon coarsely ground black pepper
1 teaspoon curry powder

Cut the cheese into fairly large pieces. Slice the onion into eight wedges. Halve the green pepper, remove the seeds and pith and cut it into chunks. Drain the pickled cucumber and slice it lengthways. Remove the rind from the bacon and cut it into fairly large pieces.

Make cuts into the sausage at 2.5-cm/1-in intervals. Place the pieces of cheese, onion, pepper, cucumber and bacon alternately in the cuts, brush the sausage and fillings generously with oil and cook over medium coals or under a moderate grill for about 15 minutes. Before serving sprinkle the sausage with the coarsely ground black pepper and curry powder. **Serves 4–6**

Serve with: Pasta and vegetable salad (page 70).

Filled sausage hats

¼ root celeriac
2 dessert apples
2 tablespoons fresh or bottled grated horseradish
1 teaspoon lemon juice
½ teaspoon sugar
pinch each of salt, paprika and ground ginger
4 tablespoons curd or cottage cheese
2–3 tablespoons single cream
8 (1-cm/½-in thick) slices Bierwurst or ham
sausage
2 tablespoons finely chopped parsley
2 tablespoons oil

Peel and grate the celeriac. Peel, halve, core and grate the apples. Mix the celeriac and apple with the horseradish, lemon juice, sugar, salt, paprika, ginger, cheese and single cream.

Cook the slices of sausage at a low heat on the barbecue or under the grill for a few minutes, until they begin to curl at the edge. Stir the parsley into the oil and brush the insides of the sausage hats several times with some of the oil mixture.

Mix the rest of the parsley oil into the filling, divide the filling between the sausage hats and serve. **Serves 4**

Serve with: Assorted breads, a green salad and a tomato or cucumber salad.

Variations
You can fill the sausage hats with a vegetable and mayonnaise salad, a rice salad or peas or asparagus tips cooked in butter, instead of the filling given above.

Swiss sausage ring

(Illustrated on pages 12–13)

3 (227-g/8-oz) smoked Dutch sausages
100 g/4 oz Emmental cheese, sliced
2 onions
225 g/8 oz streaky bacon
1 teaspoon paprika
2 tablespoons oil

Make deep cuts in the surface of the sausages at 2.5-cm/1-in intervals. Cut the cheese slices into strips 1 cm/½ in wide and 2.5 cm/1 in long. Cut each onion into eight wedges. Remove the bacon rind and slice the rashers into pieces. Mix the paprika with the oil. Fill the cuts in the sausage alternately with the cheese, onion and bacon pieces, brush the sausage and fillings generously with the paprika oil and cook on the barbecue or under the grill at a moderate heat for about 15 minutes. **Serves 6**

Serve with: Assorted breads, tomato ketchup and a mixed salad.

From the top Pasta and vegetable salad (page 70); variation of the Swiss sausage ring with peppers and gherkins.

Grilled sausage platter

100 g/4 oz back bacon
8 pork sausages
16 cocktail sausages
4 Frankfurter sausages
4 Kabanos sausages
2 Bratwurst sausages
2 beef sausages
100 g/4 oz Cheddar or Edam cheese, sliced
4 tomatoes, sliced
about 4 tablespoons oil
1 (340-g/12-oz) jar gherkins
20 stuffed olives
½ cucumber (optional)
bunch of parsley
assorted mustards and sauces
bottled creamed horseradish
tomato ketchup

Remove the rind from the bacon and cut the rashers into strips. Brush all the sausages with oil. Cut down the length of the smaller ones and fill each with small pieces of cheese and a slice of tomato. Wrap each in a strip of bacon.

Cook all the sausages at a moderate heat on the barbecue or under the grill for about 8 minutes, turning them frequently and brushing them repeatedly with oil.

Drain the gherkins and olives. Slice the cucumber, if used. Arrange the sausages on a large platter and garnish them with the gherkins, olives, cucumber, the remaining tomato and cheese slices and the parsley. Serve the sausage platter with assorted mustards and sauces, creamed horseradish and tomato ketchup. **Serves 8–10**

Serve with: Assorted breads and a green salad.

NOTE The assortment of sausages given here is intended only as a suggestion. You can of course serve whatever sausages you like.

Sausage sandwiches

8 (5-mm/¼-in thick) slices ham sausage
1 teaspoon strong mustard
2 onions
1 green pepper
2 tablespoons capers
4 slices Emmental cheese
1 tablespoon oil

Remove the skin from the sausage slices and coat them sparingly with mustard. Cut the onions into thin rings. Slice the pepper into thin rings, removing the stalk, seeds and pith. Drain the capers and crush them lightly with a fork. Finely dice the sliced cheese.

Arrange the onion and pepper rings, capers and diced cheese on four of the sausage slices and top with the remaining slices. Lightly coat both sides of the sandwiches with oil and cook them at a medium heat on the barbecue or under the grill for about 4 minutes on each side. **Serves 4**

Herby sausage kebabs

6 pork sausages with herbs
1 cucumber
16 shallots
generous pinch each of salt, garlic salt and curry powder
2 tablespoons oil

Hold the middle of each sausage in turn between thumb and forefinger and rub gently backwards and forwards, pinching it to make two short sausages. Give the sausage a final twist and cut it in half, to leave you with 12 sausages in all.

Thickly slice the cucumber. Peel the shallots. Mix the salt, garlic salt and curry powder with the oil.

Arrange the sausages, cucumber slices and shallots on four kebab skewers and brush them with the seasoned oil. Cook the kebabs over medium coals or under the grill for 10 minutes, turning them frequently and brushing them with oil. **Serves 4**

Top Grilled Sausage platter.
Bottom Herby sausage kebabs; Sausage sandwiches.

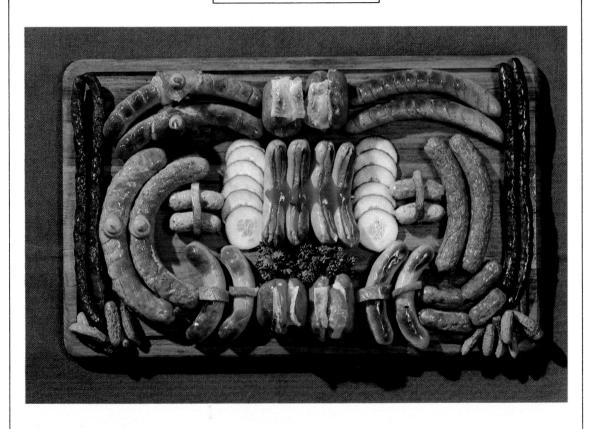

King prawn kebabs

1 (450-g/1-lb) packet frozen king prawns
350 g/12 oz fillet steak
2 green peppers
2 tablespoons oil
salt and freshly ground white pepper to taste

Allow the king prawns to thaw at room temperature, following the instructions on the packet.

Wipe the meat and cut it into even-sized cubes, removing any fat. Halve the peppers, remove the seeds and pith and cut the peppers into pieces the same size as the steak. Pat the prawns dry with absorbent kitchen paper.

Arrange the steak, prawns and green pepper alternately on four or more skewers, brush them with oil and cook the kebabs at a moderate heat on the barbecue or under the grill for 8–10 minutes. Turn them and brush them with oil frequently during cooking. Season the kebabs with salt and pepper. **Serves 4**

Serve with: French bread and Sweet corn and tomato salad (page 71).

Gourmet fish kebabs

8 fresh or frozen sole or haddock fillets
1 teaspoon lemon juice
16 canned shrimps
$\frac{1}{4}$ teaspoon salt
pinch each of pepper, paprika and dried thyme
per fish fillet
2 tomatoes
1 onion
40 g/1$\frac{1}{2}$ oz butter, melted

Separate the frozen fillets, if used, sprinkle them with lemon juice, cover and leave them to thaw following the instructions on the packet. Sprinkle fresh fish with lemon juice. Rinse the shrimps in cold water and leave to drain.

Place the fillets, skin-side down, on a flat surface. Holding the tail end of each fillet in turn in one hand, cut down the length of the fillet with a sharp knife to free the fish from the skin. Season the fish with salt, pepper, paprika and thyme, place two shrimps on each fillet, roll it up and secure with string.

Cut the tomatoes into eight wedges and the onion into thick slices. Arrange the rolled fish fillets, tomato and onion alternately on four skewers.

Grill the kebabs under a moderate heat for 10 minutes, turning frequently and sprinkling them repeatedly with melted butter. Alternatively, arrange them on a piece of cooking foil to protect them from the heat and cook them over medium coals on the barbecue. **Serves 4**

Serve with: Green salad and potatoes with parsley.

Top from the left Trout with herbs (page 31), Rump steak with tartare sauce (page 42), King prawn kebabs. *Bottom* Gourmet fish kebabs.

Cod with tomatoes

1 (1-kg/2-lb) piece of fresh cod, cleaned
½ teaspoon salt
¼ teaspoon pepper
1 teaspoon lemon juice
1 large onion
6 tomatoes
1 tablespoon oil
40 g/1½ oz butter, cut into flakes
3 tablespoons chopped fresh parsley

Rinse the fish in cold water and wipe it dry. Rub it all over with the salt, pepper and lemon juice. Cut the onion into rings and the tomatoes into thick slices.

Take a piece of cooking foil large enough to wrap the cod in and coat one side thoroughly with oil. Lay the cod on the foil, dot it with flaked butter and fold the foil around the fish, sealing well. Cook over medium coals or under the grill for 20–30 minutes on each side.

Five minutes before the end of cooking time, grill the tomato slices and onion rings lightly on the edge of the barbecue or under the grill. Unfold the edges of foil round the fish and arrange the tomato slices round it. Sprinkle onion rings and parsley over the top and serve the cod in the foil.

Serve with: Mashed potatoes or Potato and pepper salad (page 75).

Grilled salmon steaks

1.5 kg/3¼ lb cleaned tail of salmon
salt and freshly ground white pepper to taste
generous pinch of garlic salt
1 tablespoon lemon juice
4 lemons
1 cucumber
2 shallots
50 g/2 oz butter
8 tablespoons finely chopped fresh herbs
(parsley, dill and basil)

Rinse the salmon in cold water, wipe it dry and cut it into eight slices, about 2.5 cm/1 in thick. Stir the salt, pepper and garlic salt into the lemon juice and brush both sides of the salmon steaks with the mixture.

Pare the rind from one of the lemons and cut it into thin strips. Thinly slice the remaining lemons, together with the cucumber. Finely dice the shallots.

Melt the butter in a small pan and fry the diced shallots, lemon rind and chopped herbs over a low heat for a few minutes, stirring continuously. Leave the mixture to cool.

Cook the seasoned salmon steaks over medium coals or under the grill for 5–7 minutes on each side. If they begin to brown too quickly, place a piece of cooking foil on top of each, removing this however before the end of cooking time.

Arrange the grilled salmon steaks on a large flat dish interspersed with slices of cucumber and lemon. Garnish the steaks with small portions of the herb, shallot and lemon mixture. **Serves 8**

Serve with: Toast and butter and Horseradish cream (page 76) or Herb and cream cheese sauce (page 77).

Left Cod with tomatoes.
Right Grilled salmon steaks.

Cod with red wine sauce

4 (225-g/8-oz) cod steaks (middle-cut on the bone)
1 tablespoon lemon juice
salt
100 g/4 oz streaky bacon
freshly ground white pepper
2 onions
1 clove garlic
2 tomatoes
15 stuffed olives
100 g/4 oz button mushrooms
3 tablespoons olive oil
300 ml/$\frac{1}{2}$ pint red wine
1 tablespoon chopped fresh parsley
generous pinch each of dried rosemary and
dried sage
oil for grilling
GARNISH
8 lemon wedges
4 rolled anchovy fillets

Rinse the slices of cod in cold water, wipe them dry and rub them all over with lemon juice and salt. Remove the rind from the bacon and cut the rashers into short, thin strips. Pierce the cod steaks several times with a skewer and insert strips of bacon into the flesh. Sprinkle the steaks lightly with pepper.

Finely dice the onions and garlic. Cut crosses in the bases of the tomatoes, place them in a bowl containing boiling water and leave them to stand for a few minutes. Drain, peel the tomatoes and cut them into small pieces. Finely dice the olives. Trim, clean and dice the mushrooms.

Heat the olive oil in a small pan and stir-fry the onion, garlic, tomato, olives and mushrooms until soft. Pour the red wine into the pan, add the parsley, dried rosemary and sage and simmer the sauce over a gentle heat for 10–15 minutes, until reduced and thickened to taste. Season with a little salt, if liked.

Brush the cod steaks with oil and grill them over medium coals or under the grill for 15–18 minutes, turning once, until cooked. Garnish with lemon wedges and rolled anchovy fillets and serve with the red wine sauce. **Serves 4**

Cod with red wine sauce.

Halibut steaks

4 (225-g/8-oz) halibut steaks (thick middle-cuts
on the bone)
1 tablespoon lemon juice
$\frac{1}{4}$ teaspoon salt
$\frac{1}{4}$ teaspoon freshly ground pepper
few drops Tabasco sauce per steak
2 tablespoons oil

Rinse the halibut steaks in cold water and wipe them dry. Season the lemon juice with salt and pepper and rub both sides of the steaks with the mixture. Sprinkle the fish with a few drops of Tabasco and brush both sides with oil. Cook them under a medium grill or on the barbecue for 5–7 minutes on each side, brushing them repeatedly with oil. **Serves 4**

Serve with: Charcoal-baked potatoes (page 62) and Neapolitan salad (page 75).

Grilled herrings

8 cleaned, fresh herrings
2 tablespoons capers
$\frac{1}{4}$ teaspoon salt
$\frac{1}{4}$ teaspoon freshly ground pepper
$\frac{1}{2}$ teaspoon paprika
$\frac{1}{2}$ teaspoon dried rosemary
50 g/2 oz butter

Wash the fish thoroughly in cold water and wipe them dry.

Drain the capers and crush them lightly with a fork. Mix together the salt, pepper, paprika, capers and rosemary and spread this herb mixture over the insides of the herrings. Put 7 g/$\frac{1}{4}$ oz butter inside each fish. Cook the herrings over medium coals or under the grill for 10–15 minutes, turning them frequently. **Serves 8**

Serve with: Potato and pepper salad (page 75) and Creamy cucumber salad (page 76).

From the left Grilled herrings; Halibut steaks.

Plaice en papillote

4 cleaned, fresh plaice, each about 225 g/8 oz in
weight or 8 (100-g/4-oz) plaice fillets
juice of 1 lemon
½ teaspoon salt
¼ teaspoon freshly ground white pepper
150 g/5 oz streaky bacon
2 tablespoons olive oil or 40 g/1½ oz butter
8 tablespoons finely chopped fresh parsley
4 lemon wedges

Rinse the plaice thoroughly under cold running
water and wipe them dry. Season the lemon juice
with the salt and pepper and rub the mixture into
the plaice, both inside and out. Remove the rind
from the bacon, cut the rashers into strips and
then into matchsticks.

Heat the oil or butter in a frying pan and fry the
bacon, stirring continuously, until cooked. Shape
four large pieces of cooking foil into bowl shapes
and place a little of the bacon with the cooking fat
in each. Put one whole plaice or two fillets in each
foil shape and pour on the remaining bacon and
fat. Sprinkle with parsley, fold over the edges of
the foil to enclose the fish completely and seal well
with a double fold, making sure that no juices
can escape during cooking. Place the parcels under
a moderate grill or over the barbecue and cook
them for about 15 minutes, turning once.

Split open the parcels and serve the plaice on
individual plates, each with a wedge of lemon.
Serves 4

Serve with: New potatoes and Creamy cucumber
salad (page 76).

Grilled lobster

5 litres/8¾ pints water
salt and pepper
2 fresh lobsters, each about 575 g/1¼ lb in weight
100 g/4 oz butter
2 lemons, sliced

Bring the water to the boil in a large pan with
2 tablespoons salt. Plunge one lobster head first
into the boiling water, cover the pan immediately
and bring the water back to the boil. Turn down
the heat and simmer the lobster for 10 minutes.
Remove the lobster from the pan, bring the water
back to the boil and boil the second lobster in the
same way.

Place each lobster on a board and draw a sharp
knife down the centre of the back from the
shoulder to the eyes. Turn the lobster and draw the
knife in the opposite direction, from the shoulder
to the tail, cutting the lobster in two. Remove the
bright red coral or roe from each half and keep
it on one side. Discard the white gills from the
top of the head and the black intestine which runs
down the length of the tail.

Divide the butter into two portions and cut one
into flakes. Sprinkle each lobster half with a
little salt and pepper, dot it with flaked butter
and place it on the barbecue or under the grill,
cut side uppermost. Cook the lobsters at a
moderate heat for a few minutes, then turn them
over and cook the other side until it begins to
colour.

Beat the remaining butter until soft and combine
it with the reserved lobster coral. Divide the
mixture into four portions, shape each into a pat
and serve the lobsters with coral butter and lemon
slices. **Serves 2**

Grilled lobster.

Mackerel with chervil

4 cleaned mackerel
1 tablespoon lemon juice
½ teaspoon salt
¼ teaspoon freshly ground white pepper
bunch of fresh chervil or 4 teaspoons dried
chervil
25 g/1 oz butter
2 tablespoons olive oil

Rinse the mackerel thoroughly inside and out under cold running water and wipe them dry. Season the lemon juice with salt and pepper and rub the mixture into the insides of the mackerel. Place a quarter of the fresh chervil or 1 teaspoon dried chervil in the stomach cavity of each fish, together with 7 g/¼ oz butter.

Brush the mackerel with olive oil and cook them for 10–15 minutes over medium coals or under the grill, turning frequently, until golden brown. Brush them with more oil during cooking. **Serves 4**

Serve with: French bread and Herb and cream cheese sauce (page 77).

Bacon-wrapped trout

100 g/4 oz unsalted butter, softened
¾ teaspoon salt
1 teaspoon paprika
pinch of sugar
4 tablespoons tomato purée
4 cleaned, fresh trout
1 tablespoon oil
¼ teaspoon pepper
225 g/8 oz thin rashers streaky bacon

Beat the butter with ½ teaspoon salt, the paprika, sugar and tomato purée until smooth. Place the mixture on greaseproof paper or cooking foil,

Bacon-wrapped trout.

shape it into a long roll, wrap the paper or foil round it and leave it in the refrigerator until set firm.

Wash the trout thoroughly inside and out and wipe them dry. Season the oil with the remaining salt and the pepper and brush the insides of the trout with the mixture. Remove the rinds from the bacon, wrap a few rashers around each trout and hold them in place with skewers or string. Cook the trout at a low heat on the barbecue or under the grill for 15–20 minutes, until the bacon is crisp and golden brown. Turn the fish from time to time during cooking.

Cut the chilled paprika butter into slices and serve it with the trout. **Serves 4**

Serve with: Parsley tomatoes (page 60), French bread and a green salad.

Trout with herbs

(Illustrated on page 23)

2 egg yolks
¼ teaspoon celery salt
3 tablespoons oil
1 teaspoon capers
4 fresh, cleaned trout
¼ teaspoon salt
¼ teaspoon freshly ground white pepper
bunch of parsley
2 tablespoons oil

Make the sauce first. Beat the egg yolks with the celery salt and add the oil, a few drops at a time, beating continuously, to make a thick mayonnaise. Drain the capers, chop them coarsely and stir them into the sauce.

Rinse the trout carefully inside and out under cold running water and wipe them dry. Mix the salt and pepper together and rub the inside of the trout with the mixture. Place a quarter of the parsley inside each trout. Brush the fish with oil and cook them over medium coals or under the grill for 5–6 minutes on each side, brushing them repeatedly with oil. Serve at once with the mayonnaise sauce. **Serves 4**

Serve with: Boiled new potatoes and a green salad.

Stuffed sole with prawns

2 tablespoons lemon juice
2 tablespoons pineapple juice
$\frac{1}{2}$ teaspoon salt
$\frac{1}{4}$ teaspoon pepper
8 fresh or frozen sole fillets
2 (142-g/5-oz) cans prawns or 275 g/10 oz frozen prawns
$\frac{1}{4}$ cucumber
bunch of fresh dill or 2 tablespoons dried dill
25 g/1 oz butter
1 egg, beaten
2 tablespoons fresh breadcrumbs
pinch each of ground ginger and cayenne
2 tablespoons oil

Mix together the lemon and pineapple juice, the salt and pepper. Put the frozen sole fillets, if used, into a bowl, sprinkle them with the mixture, cover and leave to thaw. Place fresh fillets also into a bowl with the liquid and leave them to marinate for a few hours. Allow frozen prawns, if used, to thaw at room temperature.

Finely dice the cucumber. Finely chop the fresh dill, if used. Rinse the thawed or canned prawns in cold water, drain well and cut them into halves or quarters, depending on their size.

Melt the butter, add the diced cucumber, the fresh or dried dill and the prawns and remove the pan from the heat. Stir in the beaten egg, breadcrumbs, ginger and cayenne and mix thoroughly.

Remove the sole fillets from the marinade and wipe them dry. Spread some of the prawn mixture on each fillet, roll it up and secure it with a skewer or a wooden cocktail stick. Stir 1 tablespoon of the marinade into the oil and brush the sole fillets thoroughly with the mixture. Cook them at a medium heat on the barbecue or on an oiled tray under the grill for 10–12 minutes, turning frequently and brushing them repeatedly with the oil mixture. **Serves 4**

Serve with: French bread and Herb and cream cheese sauce (page 77).

Fish steaks with mushrooms

4 (225-g/8-oz) white fish steaks (halibut, cod, haddock)
$\frac{1}{2}$ teaspoon salt
$\frac{1}{4}$ teaspoon pepper
1 teaspoon lemon juice
1 tablespoon oil
400 g/14 oz fresh or canned button mushrooms
25 g/1 oz butter, cut into flakes
2 tablespoons finely chopped parsley

Rinse the fish steaks in cold water, wipe them dry and sprinkle them on both sides with salt, pepper and lemon juice. Grease one side of each of four large pieces of cooking foil with oil.

Clean and trim fresh mushrooms, if used, melt the butter in a pan and sauté the mushrooms for a few minutes, until soft. Drain canned mushrooms.

Place the fish steaks on the pieces of prepared foil, dot them with the butter (if you have not already used it to sauté the mushrooms) and spread the fresh or canned mushrooms on top. Fold over the edges of the foil to enclose the fish steaks completely and cook them under the grill or over medium coals for 12–15 minutes, turning once.

Open the pieces of foil, sprinkle the fish with parsley and serve them in the foil. **Serves 4**

Fish steaks with mushrooms.

Barbecued hamburgers

3 onions
1 kg/2 lb lean minced beef
1 teaspoon salt
½ teaspoon pepper

Finely dice the onions and mix them with the beef, salt and pepper. With moist hands shape the mixture into hamburgers and mark a lattice pattern on top of each with the back of a knife blade. This will help to keep them light and juicy. Place the hamburgers carefully on the barbecue or under the grill and cook them at a moderate heat for 3–7 minutes on each side, depending on whether you like them rare or well done. **Serves 8**

Serve with: Toasted white rolls or sesame buns, tomato ketchup and fried onion rings.

Gipsy porkburgers

1 egg, beaten
¼ teaspoon salt
575 g/1¼ lb minced pork
25–50 g/1–2 oz fresh breadcrumbs
generous pinch each of pepper and garlic salt
2 tablespoons oil

Work the egg and salt into the mince with enough breadcrumbs to give a smooth, not too wet mixture. Stir the pepper and garlic salt into the oil. With wet hands shape the meat mixture into burgers and brush one side of each with the seasoned oil. Cook them with the oiled side nearest the heat under a moderate grill or on the barbecue for 7 minutes, then turn, brush the other sides with oil and cook for a further 7 minutes. **Serves 4**

Serve with: Charcoal-baked potatoes (page 62) and beetroot or potato salad.

Albany cheeseburgers

(Illustrated on page 35)

1 kg/2 lb minced beef
2 eggs, beaten
½ teaspoon salt
¼ teaspoon black pepper
pinch each of dried thyme and sage
50–75 g/2–3 oz fresh breadcrumbs
2 tablespoons oil
6 slices processed Edam cheese
1 teaspoon paprika

Place the minced meat in a bowl and mix in the eggs, salt, pepper, thyme and sage. Add enough breadcrumbs to make a smooth dough, slightly firmer than for ordinary hamburgers. Form the mixture into six hand-sized hamburgers; do not make them too thick.

Brush the burgers all over with oil and cook them over medium coals or under the grill for 2 minutes on each side.

Top each burger with a slice of cheese and a sprinkling of paprika and continue to cook them until the cheese begins to melt. (The cheese will not melt as well on the barbecue as under the grill, but allow the burgers to cook at least until it begins to melt at the edges.) **Serves 6**

Serve with: Assorted breads and Creamy mustard sauce (page 77).

Hamburgers with mixed peppers

(Illustrated on page 44–45)

4 onions
575 g/1¼ lb minced beef
1 egg, beaten
½ teaspoon salt
¼ teaspoon white pepper
½ teaspoon cayenne
about 4 tablespoons fresh breadcrumbs
2 red peppers
2 green peppers
3 tablespoons oil

Finely dice two of the onions and mix them in a bowl with the minced meat, the beaten egg, salt, pepper and cayenne. Add enough breadcrumbs to give a smooth, not too moist mixture. Wet your hands, divide the mixture into four portions and shape these into large, flat hamburgers.

Slice the stalk ends off the peppers and cut the peppers into thin rings, removing the seeds and pith. Slice the remaining onions into fine rings. Brush the hamburgers and the pepper and onion rings thoroughly with oil and cook the hamburgers under the grill or over medium coals for 3–6 minutes on each side, depending on how rare you like your meat. Halfway through cooking time, add the pepper and onion rings to the barbecue or grill and cook them for a few minutes, until lightly browned. Serve each hamburger topped with a portion of mixed pepper and onion. **Serves 4**

Anchovy croquettes

1 (48-g/1¾-oz) can anchovy fillets
575 g/1¼ lb minced beef
2 eggs, beaten
¼ teaspoon salt
2 tablespoons capers
3–4 tablespoons fresh breadcrumbs
4 tablespoons dried breadcrumbs
6 green peppers
3 tablespoons oil

Rinse, drain and dice the anchovies. Place the mince

in a bowl and mix in the anchovy, half the beaten egg, the salt and capers, with enough fresh breadcrumbs to give a smooth, firm mixture. With moist hands shape the mixture into croquettes, each about 5 cm/2 in. in length. Dip these first into the remaining beaten egg and then into the dried breadcrumbs to coat thoroughly.

Trim the green peppers and cut them into quarters, removing the seeds and pith. Brush the croquettes and pepper quarters thoroughly with oil and cook them over medium coals or under the grill for about 5 minutes, turning them frequently.
Serves 4–6

Serve with: Assorted breads and a mixed salad.

Rump steak kebabs

575 g/1¼ lb rump steak
6 lamb's kidneys
1 onion
2 green peppers
2 tablespoons oil
1 tablespoon whisky
pinch each of salt, pepper and ground ginger

Wipe the meat and cut it into 1.5-cm/¾-in thick slices, removing any fat. Trim the kidneys and cut them in half. Cut the onion into eight wedges. Halve the peppers, remove the seeds and pith and cut the halves into large pieces.

Thread the slices of meat and kidney on to kebab skewers, alternating with pieces of onion and pepper. Mix the oil, whisky, salt, pepper and ground ginger together and brush the kebabs with the mixture. Cook them at a moderate heat on the barbecue or under the grill for 8–10 minutes, turning them frequently and brushing them repeatedly with the oil and whisky mixture.
Serves 4

Serve with: White bread, Mediterranean mixed salad (page 71) and grilled tomatoes sprinkled with cheese.

From the top Albany cheeseburgers (page 33); Anchovy croquettes; Barbecued chicken with paprika butter (page 49).

Sausage and steak kebabs

(Illustrated on page 38)

225 g/8 oz rump steak
4 tomatoes
100 g/4 oz button mushrooms
350 g/12 oz cocktail sausages
2 tablespoons oil
pinch of salt
generous sprinkling of freshly ground black
pepper

Wipe and trim the steak and cut it into chunks.
Halve the tomatoes. Clean and trim the mushrooms. Thread pieces of meat and tomato
alternately on to kebab skewers with the mushrooms and sausages. Mix the oil with the salt and
pepper and coat the kebabs with the mixture.
Cook them under a moderately hot grill or over
medium coals for 8–10 minutes, turning them and
brushing frequently with oil. **Serves 4**

Serve with: Potato and pepper salad (page 75).

Veal fillet kebabs

(Illustrated on page 38)

675 g/1½ lb veal fillet
4 tomatoes
½ cucumber
2 green peppers
2 tablespoons oil
generous pinch each of salt and pepper

Wipe the meat and cut it into equal cubes.
Thickly slice the tomatoes and cucumber. Halve
the peppers, remove the seeds and pith and cut
the flesh into pieces.

Arrange the pieces of meat, tomato, cucumber
and pepper alternately on kebab skewers, brush
with oil and cook the kebabs on the barbecue or
under the grill at a moderate heat for about 10
minutes, until brown and crisp. During cooking,
turn them frequently and brush them repeatedly
with oil. Season before serving.

Serve with: Creamy cucumber salad (page 76).

Shish kebab

1 (800-g/1¾-lb) shoulder or leg of lamb
8 cherry tomatoes
8 mushrooms
2 small onions
2 green peppers
4 bay leaves
6 tablespoons oil
½ teaspoon salt
¼ teaspoon pepper
1 teaspoon dried marjoram
2 teaspoons lemon juice

Wipe the meat and cut it from the bone, removing
any fat and gristle. Cut the meat into cubes about
the size of the tomatoes. Clean and trim the
mushrooms. Cut each onion into eight wedges.
Halve the peppers, remove the seeds and pith and
cut each half into four pieces. Wash the tomatoes
and place them in a bowl with the meat, mushrooms, onion, green pepper and bay leaves.

Mix the oil with the salt, pepper, marjoram and
lemon juice and pour the mixture over the meat and
vegetables. Leave to marinate in the refrigerator
for 1 hour.

Lift the meat, vegetables and bay leaves out of
the marinade and arrange them alternately on
four or six skewers. Cook the kebabs on the
barbecue or under the grill at a medium heat for
10–15 minutes, turning frequently and brushing
them repeatedly with the marinade. **Serves 4–6**

Serve with: Boiled rice.

Shish kebab.

36

Mixed sausage kebab

about 675 g/1½ lb potatoes
4 Frankfurter sausages
8 pork sausages
2 cocktail sausages
2 tablespoons oil

Scrub the potatoes, peel them if you prefer and cook them in boiling salted water for 15–20 minutes, until just tender. Drain and set them aside.

Cut the Frankfurters and pork sausages in half, first widthways, then lengthways. Halve the cocktail sausages lengthways. Slice the potatoes into halves or quarters.

Arrange the pieces of sausage and potato alternately on kebab skewers, brush them with oil and cook the kebabs on the barbecue or under the grill at a medium heat for 10 minutes, turning frequently. **Serves 4**

Serve with: A raw vegetable salad of your choice (see page 72).

Chicken liver kebabs

225 g/8 oz chicken livers
225 g/8 oz rump steak
6 tomatoes
1 (312-g/11-oz) can artichoke bottoms
pinch each of garlic salt and paprika
2 tablespoons oil

Rinse the chicken livers in cold water and pat them dry. Wipe the steak and cut it into equal chunks. Quarter the tomatoes. Drain and halve the artichoke bottoms. Mix the garlic salt and paprika into the oil.

Arrange the pieces of chicken liver, steak, tomato and artichoke alternately on four skewers. Brush the kebabs with the seasoned oil and cook them at a moderate heat on the barbecue or under the grill, turning them frequently, for 8 minutes or until they are brown and crisp. During cooking brush the kebabs repeatedly with oil. **Serves 4**

Serve with: Fresh rye or wholemeal rolls and a green salad.

Minty lamb kebabs

4 lamb cutlets
2 onions
4 tomatoes
1 tablespoon chopped fresh or 1 teaspoon dried mint
2 tablespoons oil
12 stuffed olives

Wipe the meat and cut it into even-sized pieces. Cut the onions and tomatoes into eight wedges each. Stir the mint into the oil.

Arrange the pieces of lamb, onion and tomato and the olives on four skewers and brush the kebabs with the minty oil. Cook them at a moderate heat on the barbecue or under the grill for 8–10 minutes, turning frequently. **Serves 4**

Serve with: Brown bread and French beans.

From the top Sausage and steak kebab (page 36); Veal fillet kebab (page 36); Mixed sausage kebab; Mixed pepper kebab; Chicken liver kebab; Minty lamb kebab.

Mixed pepper kebabs

225 g/8 oz pork fillet
1 red pepper
1 green pepper
1 yellow pepper
12 small gherkins
225 g/8 oz pork chipolata sausages
2 tablespoons oil
pinch each of salt and pepper

Wipe and trim the meat and cut it into equal cubes. Halve the peppers, remove the seeds and pith and cut each half into four pieces.

Drain the gherkins. Thread the meat, sausages, pepper and gherkins alternately on four kebab skewers. Season the oil with salt and pepper and brush the kebabs with the mixture. Cook them at a moderate heat on the barbecue or under the grill for about 15–20 minutes, turning frequently and brushing them repeatedly with oil. **Serves 4**

Serve with: Creamy mustard sauce (page 77), French bread and a green salad.

Porterhouse steak

250 ml/8 fl oz red wine
250 ml/8 fl oz oil
2 tablespoons fresh or 1 tablespoon dried
rosemary
2 teaspoons coarsely ground black pepper
1 clove garlic
2 (675-g/1½-lb) porterhouse steaks, about
6 cm/2½ in thick (cut from the upper part of the
sirloin)
½ teaspoon salt

Stir the red wine into the oil. Crush the rosemary with a mortar and pestle and add it to the mixture, followed by the coarsely ground pepper. Peel and crush the garlic clove and stir it also into the mixture. Wipe the meat, place it in a bowl and pour the marinade over it. Cover the bowl and leave the steak to marinate in the refrigerator for 12 hours, turning it occasionally.

Lift the steaks out of the marinade, drain them and with the point of a knife loosen the meat from the bone slightly. If there is fat round the edge of the steaks, slash through it at intervals. Grill the porterhouse steaks over hot coals for 2 minutes on each side, then move them to the edge of the barbecue where the heat is less fierce and cook each side for a further 10 minutes. Alternatively cook them under a hot grill initially, then turn the heat down to medium and continue grilling them until done. Sprinkle the steaks with salt, cut each into four portions and serve. **Serves 8**

Serve with: French bread and Sweet corn and tomato salad (page 71).

Cook's tip: If you are cooking porterhouse steaks for a special occasion, try to order them from the butcher 1–2 weeks in advance so that they will be well hung.

Pepper steak

2 tablespoons black peppercorns
4 (225-g/8-oz) rump steaks
150 ml/¼ pint oil
generous pinch of salt per steak

Crush the peppercorns with a mortar and pestle or grind them coarsely. Wipe the steaks and place them in a bowl. Mix the pepper into the oil, pour the mixture over the meat, cover the bowl and leave the steaks to marinate in the refrigerator for 5 hours, turning them in the oil from time to time.

Lift the steaks out of the oil, allow them to drain slightly and cook them over hot coals or under the grill for 3–6 minutes on each side, depending on how rare you like your steak. Season each steak with a little salt and serve. **Serves 4**

Serve with: French bread or chips and a salad.

Pepper steak.

Rump steak with tartare sauce

(Illustrated on page 23)

2 hard-boiled eggs
3 pickled cucumbers
2 tablespoons small capers
175 g/6 oz mayonnaise
6 tablespoons chopped fresh mixed herbs
(parsley, chives, thyme, marjoram)
6 tablespoons single cream
4 (225-g/8-oz) rump steaks
2 tablespoons oil
salt and freshly ground black pepper to taste

Shell and finely chop the eggs. Drain and finely dice the pickled cucumbers. Drain the capers and crush them lightly with a fork. Mix together the egg, pickled cucumber, capers, mayonnaise, herbs and cream to make a smooth sauce.

Wipe the steaks and brush them on both sides with oil. Cook them over hot coals or under the grill for 3–6 minutes on each side, depending on how rare you like your steak. Seasons with salt and pepper to taste and serve the steaks with the tartare sauce. **Serves 4**

Serve with: Mixed pickled vegetables and fresh bread rolls.

Rump steak with garlic and herb butter

(Illustrated on pages 12–13)

1 onion
2 cloves garlic
8 tablespoons chopped fresh mixed herbs
100 g/4 oz butter, softened
4 tablespoons oil
$\frac{1}{2}$ teaspoon salt
$\frac{1}{4}$ teaspoon cayenne
6 (225-g/8-oz) rump steaks

Finely dice the onion. Peel and crush the garlic. Work the herbs, garlic and onion into the butter and transfer the mixture to a small bowl.

Whisk the oil with the salt and cayenne. Wipe the steaks, brush them on both sides with the seasoned oil and cook them over hot coals or under the grill for 3–6 minutes on each side (depending on how rare you like your steak). Brush the meat repeatedly with oil during cooking. Serve with the herb butter. **Serves 6**

Serve with: French bread and a mixed salad.

Venison steaks with juniper

(Illustrated on pages 44–45)

4 (175–g/6-oz) venison steaks
1 tablespoon juniper berries
$\frac{1}{2}$ teaspoon salt
$\frac{1}{4}$ teaspoon paprika
3 tablespoons oil
pinch of dried thyme per steak

Wipe the steaks with a damp cloth. Crush the juniper berries thoroughly with a fork or a mortar and pestle. Stir the salt, paprika and juniper into the oil and brush the steaks on both sides with the mixture. Grill them over low coals or under the grill for 7–10 minutes on each side, until tender. Sprinkle with thyme before serving. **Serves 4**

Serve with: Neapolitan salad (page 75) and French bread.

Belly of pork with braised red cabbage

2 kg/4½ lb belly pork, boned and rolled
225 g/8 oz streaky bacon
5 onions
about 2 litres/3½ pints hot water
2 teaspoons sugar
1 teaspoon salt
1 tablespoon caraway seeds
2 cloves garlic, peeled
2 kg/4½ lb red cabbage
2 tablespoons oil
3 tablespoons cider vinegar
3 tablespoons demerara sugar
450 g/1 lb cooking apples
250 ml/8 fl oz beer

Rinse the pork in cold water and wipe it dry. Remove the rind from the bacon and dice the rashers. Dice all but one of the onions. Dry-fry the bacon in a large pan until the fat runs, add the diced onions and fry them until soft. Pour in the hot water, add the sugar, salt and caraway seeds and bring the water to the boil. Now add the pork with the garlic cloves – the water should just cover the meat; if it doesn't, add a little more. Simmer the pork, uncovered, for 1½ hours, then cover the pan and continue simmering for 1 hour.

Trim and shred the cabbage. Finely chop the remaining onion. Heat the oil in a large pan, add the onion and fry until transparent. Put the cabbage in the pan and continue frying for a few minutes, then add the vinegar, sugar and 3 table-spoons water. Cover the pan and simmer the cabbage gently for 1 hour, adding a little more water during cooking if necessary.

Peel, core and chop the apples. Stir them into the cabbage and continue cooking for another 30 minutes – 1 hour, until the cabbage is tender.

Lift the pork out of its cooking liquid and cut it into 2.5-cm/1-in thick slices. Allow the meat to cool, then brush it all over with beer and brown the slices over medium coals or under the grill for about 4 minutes on each side. Serve them with the red cabbage. **Serves 12**

Serve with: Red cabbage, brown bread, mustard.

Cook's tip: Don't throw away the liquid in which the pork has been cooked. It will make a wonderful stock for soups, especially split-pea or lentil.

Barbecued spare ribs

(Illustrated on pages 44–45)

2 kg/4½ lb spare rib chops
½ teaspoon each dried marjoram and dried basil
6 tablespoons oil
salt and freshly ground black pepper

Rinse the spare ribs in cold water and wipe them dry. Stir the dried marjoram and basil into the oil. Brush the spare ribs well with the oil on both sides and grill them over medium coals or under the grill for 15–20 minutes on each side, until cooked through. Brush repeatedly with oil during cooking. Sprinkle with salt and freshly ground black pepper before serving. **Serves 8**

Serve with: Barbecue sauce (page 46), brown bread and a mixed salad.

Spicy pork chops

4 slices fresh pineapple
2 tablespoons oil
4 pork chops
pinch each of pepper and dried rosemary per chop
½ teaspoon salt
2 tablespoons chutney

Peel the pineapple slices and cut out the woody centres with a circular cutter or a knife. Wipe them dry and brush them with oil.

Rub the chops on both sides with pepper, rose-mary and oil and cook them over medium coals or under the grill for 15–20 minutes on each side. Grill the pineapple rings for about 5 minutes on each side.

Season the chops with salt, arrange them on individual plates and top each with a pineapple slice. Fill the centres of the pineapple slices with a little chutney. **Serves 4**

Serve with: Fresh wholemeal or caraway seed bread.

Overleaf, top Venison steak with juniper (page 42); *centre* Barbecued spare rib (page 43); *right* Hamburger with mixed peppers (page 34); *bottom* Calf's kidneys bonne auberge (page 51).

Pork chops with prunes and apricots

(Illustrated on the front cover)

6 prunes, stoned
6 dried apricots
250 ml/8 fl oz port
4 thick pork chops with kidney, each about
175 g/6 oz in weight
a little dried basil and coarsely ground pepper
6 tablespoons water
1 teaspoon cornflour
$\frac{1}{4}$ teaspoon paprika
pinch of cayenne pepper
salt
5 tablespoons single cream
1 tablespoon oil

Soak the prunes and apricots overnight in the port.

Wipe the pork chops and cut a slit around the side of each to make a pocket. Lift the prunes and apricots out of their marinade with a straining spoon and chop them coarsely (do not discard the port). Rub the inside of the pockets in the meat with basil and pepper, divide the soaked fruit between them and secure the opening with wooden cocktail sticks.

Mix the water and port together in a pan and heat the mixture gently. Whisk in the cornflour, paprika, cayenne and salt to taste and bring to the boil, stirring continuously. Allow to boil for about 1 minute, then take the pan off the heat and stir in the cream. Keep the sauce warm.

Brush the pork chops with oil and cook them over medium coals or under the grill for 15–20 minutes on each side. Sprinkle them with a little salt and serve, accompanied by the port sauce. **Serves 4**

Serve with: French bread or potato croquettes and a green vegetable.

Pork chops with barbecue sauce

2 onions
4 tablespoons cider vinegar
300 ml/$\frac{1}{2}$ pint water
4 tablespoons brown sugar
1 tablespoon English mustard
1 teaspoon pepper
1 teaspoon salt
$\frac{1}{2}$ teaspoon cayenne
2 thick slices lemon
100 g/4 oz butter
150 ml/$\frac{1}{4}$ pint tomato ketchup
150 ml/$\frac{1}{4}$ pint tomato purée
2 teaspoons Worcestershire sauce
6 pork chops
2 tablespoons oil
generous pinch of salt per chop

Dice the onions and mix them in a pan with the vinegar, water, sugar, mustard, pepper, salt and cayenne. Add the lemon slices, bring the mixture to the boil and simmer it over a low heat for 20 minutes.

Remove the pan from the heat and stir in the butter until it melts. Add the tomato ketchup, tomato purée and Worcestershire sauce, stir well and bring the sauce to the boil once more over a low heat. Cover the pan and keep it hot on the edge of the barbecue or on top of your cooker.

Wipe the pork chops and slash the fat round the edge of each at 2.5-cm/1-in intervals. Brush the chops with oil and cook them over hot coals or under the grill for 4 minutes on each side. Then turn down the heat to medium, or raise the meat further from the coals, and cook the chops for a further 10–12 minutes on each side, until well done.

Season the chops with a little salt and serve them with the barbecue sauce. **Serves 6**

Serve with: French bread, Potato and pepper salad (page 75) and a green or vegetable salad.

Pork chops with barbecue sauce.

Hungarian paprika chops

(Illustrated on pages 12–13)

6 pork chops
1½ teaspoons paprika
3 tablespoons oil

Wipe the chops and slash the fat round the edge of each at 1-cm/½-in intervals. Stir the paprika into the oil and brush the chops thoroughly with the mixture. Cook the chops over medium coals or under the grill for 15–20 minutes on each side, until well done. **Serves 6**

Serve with: Assorted breads, pickled cucumber and mixed pickled vegetables.

Chicken legs à l'Arles

6 tablespoons oil
3 tablespoons white wine
generous pinch each of salt and pepper
1 teaspoon dried rosemary
8 chicken legs

In a pan whisk together the oil, white wine, salt, pepper and rosemary. Bring the mixture to the boil and take the pan off the heat. Wipe the meat, put it in a large bowl and pour over the hot liquid. Cover and leave to marinate for 1 hour.

Lift the chicken legs out of the marinade, wipe them dry and lay them on the grill pan or barbecue. Cook them over low coals or under the grill for 25 minutes, turning the legs every 5 minutes and brushing them with the marinade. **Serves 8**

Serve with: Potato salad with fresh herbs and mayonnaise.

Barbecued chicken with paprika butter

(Illustrated on page 35)

6 chicken quarters
1 teaspoon salt
¼ teaspoon pepper
150 ml/¼ pint oil
3 tablespoons lemon juice
2 teaspoons mustard
1½ teaspoons paprika
100 g/4 oz butter, softened
1 red pepper

Wipe the chicken quarters and place them in a large bowl. Whisk together the salt, pepper, oil, lemon juice and mustard, pour the mixture over the chicken, cover and leave to marinate for 2 hours. During this time turn the chicken in the marinade from time to time.

Mix the paprika with the softened butter. Cut the red pepper in half, remove the seeds and pith and finely dice the flesh. Work the diced pepper into the paprika butter, shape the butter into a long roll and wrap it in a piece of cooking foil. Leave it to set in the refrigerator until required.

Remove the chicken quarters from the marinade and wipe them dry. Cook them over medium coals or under the grill for 15–20 minutes on each side, until crisp and tender. Brush them frequently with the marinade during cooking.

Cut the paprika butter into slices and serve it with the grilled chicken. **Serves 6**

Serve with: French bread and a mixed salad.

Turkey drumsticks and escalopes

2 turkey drumsticks
4 (175-g/6-oz) turkey escalopes
1 teaspoon salt
½ teaspoon dried marjoram
½ teaspoon black pepper
about 3 tablespoons oil
pinch of cayenne

Wipe all the meat and rub the drumsticks thoroughly with half the salt, the marjoram and black pepper. Grease two large pieces of cooking foil with oil and wrap the drumsticks in them loosely, sealing the edges well. Cook the turkey i the foil over medium coals or under the grill for about 45 minutes, turning occasionally.

Rub both sides of the turkey escalopes with oil and cook them over medium coals or under the grill for 5–7 minutes on each side, until well done.

Remove the drumsticks from the foil, brush them with the rest of the oil and brown them over the coals or under the grill for a few minutes until crisp and golden.

Sprinkle the turkey escalopes with the remaining salt and the cayenne and serve them with the drumsticks. **Serves 8**

Serve with: Avocado sauce (page 77), Parsley tomatoes (page 60), lemon wedges, parsley sprigs and green salad.

Turkey drumsticks and escalopes.

Special mixed grill

4 lamb chops
8 bacon rashers
20 mushrooms
2 tomatoes
bunch of parsley
8 sausages
3 tablespoons oil
salt and coarsely ground black pepper
generous pinch of dried sage

Wipe the lamb chops. Remove the rind from the bacon, roll up the rashers and secure them with wooden cocktail sticks. Clean and trim the mushrooms. Cut the tomatoes in half. Wash and drain the parsley and divide it into sprigs.

Brush the chops, bacon, mushrooms, tomatoes and sausages with oil. Cook the chops over medium coals or under the grill for 8–10 minutes on each side, brushing them frequently with oil. Halfway through cooking time, put the sausages, bacon, mushrooms and tomatoes on to grill and cook them until the bacon and sausages are done and the vegetables nicely browned. Turn and brush them with oil during cooking.

Season all the cooked ingredients with salt and pepper and sprinkle the tomatoes with the sage. Arrange the mixed grill on a large serving platter and garnish it with sprigs of parsley. **Serves 4**

Calf's kidneys bonne auberge

(Illustrated on pages 44–45)

4 whole calf's kidneys
150 g/5 oz streaky bacon
1 onion
salt and white pepper
$\frac{1}{2}$ teaspoon paprika

Halve the kidneys lengthways, remove any veins, wash them in cold water and wipe them dry. Remove the rind from the bacon and cut the rashers in half. Slice the onion into rings.

Rub the cut sides of the kidneys with salt. Place the bacon rashers on the barbecue or grill pan and lay the kidneys, cut-side down, on top. Cook the kidneys over low coals or under the grill for 8–10 minutes, turn them and continue grilling for a further 8–10 minutes until cooked through.

Meanwhile grill the onion rings lightly on both sides on the edge of the barbecue or grill pan. Sprinkle the kidneys with pepper and paprika and serve them with the bacon and onion rings.
Serves 8

Serve with: Parsley tomatoes (page 60) and French bread or chips.

Cook's tip: If you are lucky enough to be able to obtain kidneys still encased in their own fat, you can do without the bacon. Simply halve the kidneys, sprinkle the cut sides with salt and grill them over the barbecue or under the grill as above. Trim away the fat when the kidneys are cooked and serve.

Grilled liver with apple

$\frac{1}{2}$ teaspoon white pepper
pinch of dried marjoram
2 tablespoons oil
2 dessert apples
$\frac{1}{2}$ teaspoon honey
1 tablespoon beer
4 thin slices calf's or ox liver, each about
225 g/8 oz in weight
$\frac{1}{2}$ teaspoon salt

Whisk the pepper and marjoram into the oil. Peel and slice the apples and remove the cores. Mix the honey and beer together. Wipe the liver, brush it with the seasoned oil and cook the slices over medium coals or under the grill for 3–5 minutes on each side. Coat the apple slices with the beer and honey mixture and grill them, too, for 4 minutes on each side. Sprinkle the cooked liver with a little salt and arrange it on individual plates, topped with the apple slices. **Serves 4**

Special mixed grill.

Mixed grill platter

2 lamb chops
2 veal chops
2 pork chops
1 (450-g/1-lb) pork fillet
450 g/1 lb chicken livers
2 gammon steaks
about 4 tablespoons oil
4 canned pineapple rings
8 tomatoes
salt and pepper
$\frac{1}{2}$ teaspoon paprika
pinch of garlic salt
$\frac{1}{2}$ teaspoon dried rosemary
2 tablespoons grated Parmesan cheese

Wipe all the meat and slash through the fat round the edges of the chops at intervals. Cut the pork fillet into slices. Trim the chicken livers. Brush all the pieces of meat thoroughly with oil and cook them over medium coals or under the grill until well done. The gammon, pork fillet and pork chops will need 15–20 minutes on each side; the veal chops, 10–12 minutes on each side and the lamb chops, about 10 minutes on each side. Put the chicken livers on to cook last of all as these should be done after 8–10 minutes in all. Turn them occasionally so that they are evenly cooked.

While the meat is cooking, grill the pineapple rings on both sides on the edge of the barbecue or the grill pan, together with the tomatoes. Season all the meat with salt and pepper and sprinkle the pork fillet with paprika, the lamb with garlic salt and the veal with rosemary. Arrange the meat on a large serving platter and garnish with the pineapple rings. Sprinkle the tomatoes with Parmesan and place them on the dish. **Serves 8–10**

Serve with: Chips, green peas and French beans cooked in butter and assorted breads.

Mixed grill platter.

Crispy knuckle of pork

1 knuckle of pork, about 2.5 kg/5½ lb in weight
½ teaspoon marjoram
½ teaspoon salt
½ teaspoon ground caraway seeds
3 tablespoons oil
1 tablespoon honey
1 tablespoon hot water

Wipe the meat and skewer it on the roasting spit along the bone, making sure that the prongs at each end of the spit are firmly holding the meat. For extra security, fasten the meat with kitchen string. Cook the pork over medium coals, rotating the spit continuously, for 2–3 hours, until well done. Check this with a meat thermometer if you like: the temperature at the centre of the meat should have reached 85 C (185 F).

Whisk the marjoram, salt and caraway into the oil. After 40 minutes of cooking time, brush the pork repeatedly with the seasoned oil. About 15 minutes before the end of cooking time, stir the honey into the hot water and brush the pork with the mixture.

Take the pork off the spit and allow it to rest for 5–10 minutes before carving. **Serves 6**

Serve with: Charcoal-baked potatoes (page 62) and a raw vegetable salad (page 72).

Belly of pork with apple

3 onions
450g/1 lb small dessert apples
½ teaspoon salt
¼ teaspoon pepper
1 (1-kg/2¼-lb) piece of boned belly pork
10 cloves
½ teaspoon ground cinnamon
50g/2 oz butter
1½ tablespoons brown sugar

Quarter the onions. Peel, quarter and core the apples. Mix together the salt and pepper and rub the seasoning into the pork. Stick the cloves into the pieces of apple and sprinkle all the apple with ground cinnamon.

Cut half the butter into flakes. Spread the pieces of onion and apple over the meat and dot them with the flaked butter. Roll up the meat and tie it securely with string, sealing the ends as well as the join of the roll.

Skewer the joint on to a large spit, fix it firmly in place and cook it on the rôtisserie over medium coals for about 1½ hours, until well done and the centre of the joint has reached a temperature of 85 C (185 F) – you can check this on a meat thermometer if you have one. Melt the remaining butter in a pan on the barbecue, stir in the sugar and for the last 30 minutes of cooking time brush the joint with this mixture. **Serves 4–6**

Grilled spare rib of pork

(Illustrated on pages 54–55)

2 kg/4½ lb spare rib or blade of pork, boned and rolled
2 teaspoons salt
¼ teaspoon freshly ground white pepper
½ teaspoon curry powder
2 teaspoons paprika
4 tablespoons oil

Wipe the meat and skewer it on to a large spit. Mix the salt with all the spices and rub the seasoning well into the meat. Brush the joint thoroughly with oil.

Cook the pork over medium coals, rotating the spit continuously and brushing the meat occasionally with oil, for 2–3 hours, until cooked. If you have a meat thermometer you can check when the meat is ready; the temperature at the centre of the pork should have reached 85 C (185 F). **Serves 6–8**

Serve with: Grilled pineapple and apple slices and a potato or raw vegetable salad (page 72).

Overleaf Grilled spare rib of pork.

Roast stuffed sucking-pig

1 oven-ready sucking-pig, about 5 kg/11 lb in
weight
2 onions
1½ teaspoons salt
1 bay leaf
175 g/6 oz coarse fresh breadcrumbs
100 g/4 oz sausagemeat
2 teaspoons black pepper
50 g/2 oz shelled pistachio nuts (optional)
2–3 eggs, beaten
250 ml/8 fl oz oil
250 ml/8 fl oz beer

Ask your butcher to give you the heart, tongue and
liver of the sucking-pig to make the stuffing.

Wash the heart and tongue and place them in a pan
with 1 onion, 1 teaspoon salt and the bay leaf.
Pour in enough water to cover, put the lid on the
pan, bring to the boil and simmer for 30 minutes.
Dice the second onion.

Drain the cooked heart and tongue and mince
them very finely with the liver and diced onion.
Stir in the breadcrumbs, sausagemeat, the remaining salt, the pepper and pistachios, if used,
and add enough beaten egg to bind the ingredients
to a soft, not too moist mixture.

Wipe the inside of the sucking-pig with absorbent
kitchen paper, put in the stuffing and sew up the
opening with a trussing needle and string. Tie
the front legs securely alongside the head and the
back legs under the stomach. Skewer the pig on to
a large spit, running the spit as close to the back-
bone as possible and securing the pig well with
the forks at each end of the spit. Wrap the ears
and trotters in cooking foil to protect them from
the heat, brush the whole pig with oil and cook it
on the rôtisserie over medium coals for 4–5 hours,
brushing it with oil from time to time.

During the last 30 minutes of cooking time, brush
the pig all over with beer. Serve it on a large
wooden platter and carve it at the table.
Serves 10–12

Serve with: Assorted fresh breads and a raw
vegetable salad (page 72).

Spit-roast leg of lamb with mint sauce

2 sprigs of fresh rosemary
2 sprigs of fresh sage
250 ml/8 fl oz oil
8 tablespoons finely chopped fresh mint
2 tablespoons sugar
3 tablespoons hot water
150 ml/¼ pint wine vinegar
3 cloves garlic
1 (2–2.5 kg/4½–5½ lb) leg of lamb
1 teaspoon salt
1 teaspoon freshly ground pepper

Put the fresh rosemary and sage in a bowl with the
oil, cover and leave to marinate in the refrigerator
for at least 3 days.

Shortly before you are ready to cook, wash, dry
and finely chop the mint leaves. Dissolve the sugar
in the hot water. Put the mint in a sauceboat,
pour in the hot liquid followed by the vinegar,
stir well and leave to stand.

Peel the garlic and cut the cloves into thin slivers.
Wipe the leg of lamb, pierce the skin in several
places and insert the slivers of garlic into the holes.

Skewer the lamb on to the rôtisserie spit so that
the spit runs almost parallel with the bone. Brush
the meat all over with the rosemary and sage oil
and cook it over medium coals for 2–2½ hours,
rotating the spit continuously and brushing the
meat repeatedly with oil, until cooked through.
You can check by inserting a meat thermometer
into the centre of the meat; the temperature should
have reached 70 C (160 F) for medium done lamb
or 80 C (180 F) for well done.

When the meat is cooked, remove the leg from the
spit, place it on a wooden board and leave it to
stand for at least 10 minutes to allow all the
juices to settle. Sprinkle it well with salt and
pepper, carve it into slices and serve the mint
sauce alongside. **Serves 6–8**

Serve with: French beans cooked in butter and
French bread.

Spit-roast leg of lamb with mint sauce.

Spit-roast beef sirloin

1 kg/2¼ lb beef sirloin
2 tablespoons oil
½ teaspoon salt
¼ teaspoon white pepper

Wipe the meat and fasten it firmly on a large spit, making sure that the forks at each end grip the joint firmly. Brush it all over with oil and roast it over medium to hot coals, rotating the spit continuously, for 35–45 minutes, depending on how rare you want it to be. Brush it with oil from time to time during cooking.

Season the beef with salt and pepper and leave it to stand for 5–10 minutes before carving to give the juices time to settle. **Serves 4**

Serve with: Herb tomatoes (page 60) or Neapolitan salad (page 75) and Garlic bread (page 64).

Giant fillet kebab

225 g/8 oz beef fillet
225 g/8 oz veal fillet
450 g/1 lb pork fillet
4 courgettes
4 tomatoes
2 small onions
4 mild fresh chillies
½ teaspoon salt
¼ teaspoon pepper
pinch of garlic salt
3 tablespoons oil

Wipe all the meat, remove any fat and cut the pieces of fillet into fairly large, equal-sized cubes. Cut the courgettes into large chunks. Halve the tomatoes and peel the onions.

Skewer the pieces of fillet and courgette, the tomatoes, onions and chillies on to a large spit. Stir the salt, pepper and garlic salt into the oil and brush the kebab with the mixture. Cook it on the rôtisserie over medium coals for 20–25 minutes (depending on the size of the pieces of meat). **Serves 4**

Serve with: French bread and Mediterranean mixed salad (page 71).

Spit-roast duck with orange

1 oven-ready duck, about 2 kg/4½ lb in weight
½ teaspoon salt
¼ teaspoon pepper
½ teaspoon paprika
1 small orange

Rinse the duck inside and out with cold water and wipe it dry. Mix together the salt, pepper and paprika and rub the mixture well into the inside of the bird. Wash and dry the orange and place it in the duck. Skewer the duck securely lengthways on the rôtisserie spit, making sure the spit also passes through the orange and that the forks on each end of the spit are firmly embedded in the meat. Fasten the wings and legs to the body of the duck with kitchen string or skewers and roast it over medium coals, rotating the spit continuously, for 1–2 hours. It will be ready when the temperature at the centre of the meat has reached 90 C/190 F – you can check this with a meat thermometer.

Remove the duck from the spit and carve it into four portions. **Serves 4**

Serve with: French bread, apple sauce and glazed turnips or Braised red cabbage (page 43).

Giant fillet kebab.

Grilled accompaniments

Parsley tomatoes

8 medium tomatoes
pinch each of salt and pepper per tomato
2 tablespoons oil
2 tablespoons chopped parsley

Remove the stalks from the tomatoes and cut a cross into the base of each. Sprinkle the tomatoes with salt and pepper and cook them, cross-side downwards, under a hot grill or on the barbecue for 5 minutes, brushing them repeatedly with oil. Turn the tomatoes over and continue grilling for a further 5 minutes. Sprinkle a little parsley on each tomato and serve. **Serves 8**

Serve with: Fish, poultry and meat (especially steak). Grilled tomatoes are great favourites with all kinds of dishes, as grilling preserves all their individual flavour.

Barbecued corn on the cob

4 corn cobs
1 tablespoon oil
$\frac{1}{2}$ teaspoon salt
$\frac{1}{2}$ teaspoon paprika
75 g/3 oz butter

Remove any leaves and fibres from the corn cobs, place them in boiling salted water and simmer them for 15 minutes. Drain and allow to cool slightly.

Season the oil with salt and paprika and brush the cobs all over with the mixture. Cook them over medium coals or under the grill for 10–15 minutes, turning frequently. During cooking brush the corn repeatedly with the seasoned oil.

Stick corn cob holders into the ends of the cobs, if liked, and serve each with a knob of butter. **Serves 4**

Herb tomatoes

8 tomatoes
$\frac{1}{2}$ teaspoon salt
$\frac{1}{4}$ teaspoon pepper
1 tablespoon oil
1 teaspoon dried sage
2 tablespoons chopped fresh parsley

Cut the tomatoes in half. Mix the salt and pepper into the oil. Brush the tomatoes and the grill or grill pan well with the oil and cook the tomatoes on the barbecue or under the grill, cut side down, for 2 minutes. Turn them over and cook them for a further 3 minutes, until lightly browned. Sprinkle with sage and chopped parsley and serve. **Serves 8**

Parsley tomatoes.

Right Barbecued corn on the cob; Herb tomatoes.

Charcoal-baked potatoes

8 large potatoes
2 teaspoons salt
2 tablespoons oil
225 g/8 oz Garlic and herb butter (page 42)

Wash the potatoes well and wipe them dry. Cut a cross into the side of each and rub the whole potato with salt. Brush eight pieces of cooking foil with oil and wrap the potatoes tightly inside. Place the potatoes in foil directly on the barbecue coals (at the side of the barbecue rather than the centre) and bake them for 50–60 minutes, until tender. Turn them from time to time.

Remove the cooked potatoes from the coals and squeeze them lightly to make sure they are cooked and soft. Top each potato with a generous helping of Garlic and herb butter and serve them with teaspoons. **Serves 8**

Variations

Try these other fillings instead of the herb butter, or serve them alongside .

Spicy onion and liver sausage filling

2 onions
2 cloves garlic
1 tablespoon capers
2 strips canned pimiento
225 g/8 oz liver sausage
2 tablespoons chopped fresh mixed herbs
1 teaspoon paprika

Finely chop the onions. Peel and crush the garlic. Drain and chop the capers and pimiento. Mash the liver sausage with all the ingredients and put a little of the filling in each potato.

Sour cream and mock caviare filling

300 ml/$\frac{1}{2}$ pint soured cream
2 tablespoons chopped fresh chives
8 teaspoons red or black lumpfish roe

Stir the cream lightly until smooth and mix in the chopped chives. Divide the cream between the potatoes and top with a teaspoon of lumpfish roe.

Potato and bacon skewers

4 medium potatoes
2 large onions
225 g/8 oz streaky bacon
1 tablespoon oil
1 teaspoon caraway seeds

Peel the potatoes and cut them into thick slices together with the onions. Remove the rind from the bacon and cut the rashers into pieces. Stir the caraway seeds into the oil. Arrange the slices of potato, onion and bacon on four skewers, brush them well with the caraway oil and cook them over medium coals or under the grill for 15–18 minutes, turning frequently and brushing them with oil. **Serves 4**

Stuffed cucumbers

4 hard-boiled eggs
350 g/12 oz boiled ham, unsliced
2 cooked potatoes
4 small, thick cucumbers
2 tablespoons chopped fresh parsley
4 tablespoons single cream or natural yogurt
1 teaspoon mustard
$\frac{1}{2}$ teaspoon sugar
1 teaspoon lemon juice
salt and pepper
2 tablespoons oil

Shell the eggs and dice them, together with the ham and potatoes. Slice the cucumbers in half lengthways and scrape out the seeds with a teaspoon. Cut out small pieces of the cucumber flesh and mix them with the egg, ham and potato. Make a dressing with the parsley, cream or yogurt, mustard, sugar, lemon juice and seasoning to taste and stir this into the egg and ham mixture. Fill four of the cucumber halves with the mixture and top with the remaining halves.

Brush four large pieces of cooking foil with oil and wrap the cucumbers in them. Cook over low to medium coals or under the grill for 20–25 minutes, turning frequently. **Serves 4**

Top Charcoal-baked potatoes.
Bottom Stuffed cucumbers.

Stuffed courgettes

4 large courgettes
1 onion
3 tablespoons oil
350 g / 12 oz minced beef
50 g / 2 oz fresh breadcrumbs
1 small egg, beaten
½ teaspoon salt
¼ teaspoon pepper
½ teaspoon paprika

Halve the courgettes lengthways and scrape out the seeds with a teaspoon. Remove some of the flesh from each half and put this on one side.

Finely dice the onion. Heat 2 tablespoons of the oil in a pan ond fry the onion until soft. Add the minced beef and continue frying, stirring occasionally, for 10–15 minutes, until the meat is cooked. Take the pan off the heat and stir in the courgette flesh followed by the breadcrumbs, beaten egg, salt, pepper and paprika.

Fill the courgettes with the minced meat mixture and put the halves together again. Use the remaining oil to grease four pieces of cooking foil and wrap the courgettes inside. Cook them over medium coals or under the grill, turning occasionally, for 20–30 minutes. **Serves 4**

Garlic bread

(Illustrated on the front cover)

1 French loaf
2 or more cloves garlic
¼ teaspoon salt
4 tablespoons chopped fresh mixed herbs
100 g / 4 oz butter, softened

Make cuts all along the French loaf at 2.5-cm / 1-in intervals, but do not slice all the way through. Peel and crush the garlic cloves. Work the salt, garlic and herbs into the butter until smooth and spread the cuts in the bread with the mixture. Wrap the loaf in a large piece of cooking foil and cook it over medium coals or in a moderately hot oven (200 C, 400 F, gas 6) for 15 minutes, turning once. Unwrap the loaf and serve hot. **Serves 4**

Raclette

Raclette is a Swiss speciality, made by holding a large piece of the local semi-hard cheese over the fire until it begins to melt and scraping off the softened part on to a plate. A barbecue is just the right occasion for it, served with baked potatoes.

½ whole semi-hard cheese (Gruyère, Fontina)
8–10 Charcoal-baked potatoes (page 62)
2 tablespoons coarse salt

Place the cheese over hot coals with the cut surface directly touching the barbecue grill. As soon as a layer of cheese has melted, use a sharp knife to scrape it off on to a plate and serve it with a potato and some coarse salt.

NOTE You will find this a fairly time-consuming meal as each portion of cheese has to be melted and served separately. You can always cheat by cutting the cheese into serving portions first and melting these all together on the barbecue or under the grill. **Serves 8–10**

Mixed vegetable kebabs

(Illustrated on the front cover)

2 peppers (red, yellow or green)
2 large courgettes
8 shallots
12 button mushrooms
8 cherry tomatoes
8 bay leaves
a few fresh sage leaves (optional)
2 tablespoons oil

Slice the stalks off the peppers and cut the flesh into large pieces, removing the seeds and pith. Trim the courgettes and cut them into chunks. Peel the shallots. Clean and trim the mushrooms. Thread the pieces of pepper and courgette, the shallots, mushrooms and tomatoes on to kebab skewers, alternating them with the bay leaves and sage, if used. Brush all the vegetables well with oil and cook the kebabs over medium coals or under the grill for about 10 minutes, turning once. Brush them with more oil during cooking. **Serves 4**

Raclette.

Stuffed rum apples

2 tablespoons sultanas
4 large dessert apples
75 g/3 oz butter
100 g/4 oz ground hazelnuts
175 g/6 oz biscuit crumbs
1½ tablespoons rum
1½ tablespoons lemon juice
4 heaped tablespoons brown sugar

Put the sultanas in a bowl with lukewarm water and leave them to soak. Wash and dry the apples and remove the cores with an apple corer or a sharp knife. Cut a slice off the top of each apple, peel this and chop the flesh. Alternatively, cut out some of the flesh from inside the apple, leaving a large cavity in each. Melt the butter but do not allow it to brown. Mix 3 tablespoons of the melted butter with the chopped apple, the ground hazelnuts, biscuit crumbs, rum, lemon juice and sugar. Drain the sultanas and stir them into the mixture.

Press the filling firmly into the four apples, brush them with the remaining butter and place them on a piece of cooking foil. Cook the apples under a moderate grill for 12 minutes, turning them from time to time, until they are golden brown all over. Alternatively, wrap each apple completely in foil, place it directly on the barbecue over low to medium coals and cook it for 8 minutes, turning occasionally. **Serves 4**

Pineapple annabelle

1 fresh pineapple
50 g/2 oz butter
2 tablespoons sugar
4 tablespoons banana liqueur
4 tablespoons whipped cream (optional)

Peel the pineapple and cut it into slices, about 2.5 cm/1 in thick. Cut out the woody centre of each slice with a sharp knife. Melt the butter. Brush the pineapple rings all over with half the butter and cook them on an oiled grill over medium coals or under the grill for 4 minutes.

Brush the remaining butter over the pineapple rings, sprinkle them with half the sugar, turn and cook them for a further 4 minutes. Before serving, scatter the remaining sugar over the pineapple and pour on the banana liqueur. Fill the centre of each slice with a tablespoon of whipped cream, if used. **Serves 4**

NOTE This delicious dessert will also make a very good accompaniment with grilled chicken, gammon steaks and game if you omit the banana liqueur and whipped cream.

Bananas with maple syrup

4 bananas, peeled
1 tablespoon lemon juice
2 tablespoons maple syrup
50 g/2 oz butter
4 teaspoons brown sugar
1 teaspoon cinnamon

Halve the bananas lengthways. Stir the lemon juice into the maple syrup. Brush the bananas with the syrup and place the halves together again. Melt the butter. Brush four pieces of cooking foil with butter, place a banana on each and sprinkle any remaining butter over the top. Fold the pieces of foil round the bananas, seal the edges and cook them over medium coals or under the grill for 10 minutes, turning from time to time.

Open out the foil and sprinkle each banana with a little brown sugar and cinnamon before serving. **Serves 4**

Stuffed rum apples.

Cinnamon apple rings

4 large, firm dessert apples
juice of 1 lemon
50 g/2 oz butter, melted
4 tablespoons sugar
2 tablespoons cinnamon

Thinly peel the apples, remove the cores with an apple corer and cut the fruit into rings, about 1 cm/½ in thick. Sprinkle both sides of the rings with lemon juice and drain them slightly on absorbent kitchen paper. Now brush the rings with half the melted butter and cook them over low coals on the edge of the barbecue or under the grill for 3 minutes.

Mix together the sugar and cinnamon and sprinkle some of the mixture on the upper sides of the apple rings. Turn the rings, brush the undersides with the remaining melted butter, sprinkle them with more of the cinnamon mixture and grill them for a further 3 minutes. Give the apples a final coating of the cinnamon mixture just before serving. If you like, you can mix an additional quantity of sugar and cinnamon and serve it with the apples. **Serves 4**

Cinnamon apple rings.

Cranberry peaches

4 fresh peaches or 8 canned peach halves
50 g/2 oz butter
1 tablespoon lemon juice
1 tablespoon crème de cassis
2 tablespoons cranberry sauce

Cut fresh peaches in half and remove the stones. Drain canned peaches. Melt the butter and brush it all over the peach halves, then cook them on the barbecue over medium coals or under the grill for 3 minutes on each side.

Stir the lemon juice and liqueur into the cranberry sauce and spoon a little of the mixture into the centre of each peach half before serving.

Ginger Pears

4 ripe pears
8 pieces preserved stem ginger
½ lemon
1 tablespoon syrup from the ginger jar
1 tablespoon sugar
1 tablespoon Williamine or Kirsch liqueur
2 teaspoons cinnamon

Cut the pears in half and scoop out the cores. Place each pear half on a piece of kitchen foil and fold the foil up around it to form a kind of bowl, but do not totally enclose the pears.

Slice the pieces of ginger root into fine strips. Thinly peel the lemon and cut the rind into similar strips. Squeeze the lemon juice and stir it into the ginger syrup with the strips of ginger and lemon, the sugar and the Williamine or Kirsch.

Cook the pear halves in their pieces of foil over medium coals for 5 minutes. Then remove the foil, place the pears directly on the grill, cut-side down, and continue cooking for 3 minutes. Alternatively, cook the pears without any foil under a medium grill for 5 minutes, then turn up the temperature to hot and grill them for a further 3 minutes.

Fill the centres of the grilled pears with the lemon and ginger mixture and sprinkle a little cinnamon over the top. **Serves 4**

Maraschino oranges

2 large oranges
1 teaspoon clear honey
2 tablespoons maraschino or Kirsch liqueur
4 maraschino cherries

Cut the oranges in half, place each half on a piece of cooking foil and fold the foil up around it to form a sort of bowl. Stir the honey into the maraschino or Kirsch.

Cook the oranges in the foil over hot coals for 5 minutes, then remove the foil, turn the oranges over and cook them with the cut sides directly touching the grill for a further 3 minutes. You can also simply grill them without any foil under a medium grill for 5 minutes, then turn up the heat to hot and continue cooking for a further 3 minutes.

Sprinkle the oranges immediately with the honey and liqueur mixture and top each with a maraschino cherry. **Serves 4**

Fruit salad kebabs

2 oranges
2 dessert apples
1 dessert pear
2 fresh peaches or 4 canned peach halves
1 (227-g/8-oz) can pineapple pieces
2 bananas

Peel the oranges, removing as much of the pith as you can and cut them into thick slices. Quarter and core the apples and pear and cut the quarters into chunks. Halve the fresh peaches, if used, remove the stones and cut the fresh or canned peach halves into large pieces. Drain the canned pineapple, reserving the juice. Cut the bananas into chunks.

Thread all the pieces of fruit alternately on to kebab skewers and brush them well with the pineapple juice. Cook the kebabs over medium coals or under the grill for about 5 minutes and serve them hot with cream or ice cream. **Serves 4**

Ginger pears (page 68) ; Maraschino oranges.

Mexican salad

4 green peppers
2 cucumbers
4 sticks celery
4 large tomatoes
1 (425-g/15-oz) can kidney beans
5 tablespoons oil
3 tablespoons wine vinegar
1 tablespoon bottled chilli sauce
¼ teaspoon salt
generous pinch of black pepper

Halve the peppers, remove the seeds and pith and dice the flesh. Peel the cucumbers, cut them in half lengthways, scoop out the seeds with a teaspoon and cut the flesh into small cubes. Trim and slice the celery, keeping the youngest leaves on one side. Quarter the tomatoes. Drain the kidney beans. Mix all these ingredients together in a bowl.

Make a dressing from the oil, vinegar, chilli sauce, salt and pepper and pour it over the salad. Chop the celery leaves and sprinkle them over the top. Cover the salad and leave it to stand at room temperature for 30 minutes. **Serves 8–10**

Pasta and vegetable salad

(Illustrated on page 19)

350 g/12 oz macaroni or pasta shells
175 g/6 oz frozen peas
2 strips canned pimiento
3 pickled cucumbers
2 small onions
225 g/8 oz salami
3 tablespoons oil
1½ tablespoons wine vinegar
½ teaspoon salt
¼ teaspoon pepper
bunch of parsley, finely chopped

Cook the pasta in boiling salted water for about 15 minutes, following the instructions on the packet. Bring a very little water to the boil in a separate pan, add the peas, cover and simmer them over a low heat for 6 minutes.

Drain and dice the pimiento and pickled cucumbers. Dice the onions. Remove the rind from the salami and cut the meat into strips.

Drain the peas and pasta, rinse the pasta through with cold water and leave it to dry. Mix the peas, pasta, diced pimiento, cucumber, onion and salami together in a bowl. Whisk the oil with the vinegar, salt, pepper and parsley, stir the dressing into the salad, cover and leave it to stand for a few minutes. **Serves 6–8**

Smoked ham salad

2 eggs
½ cucumber
1 lettuce
4 tomatoes
225 g/8 oz smoked ham
20 stuffed olives
250 ml/8 fl oz Mayonnaise (page 76)

Hard boil the eggs for 10 minutes, plunge them into cold water, shell and cut them into slices. Thinly slice the cucumber. Wash the lettuce, separate it into leaves and allow to drain. Cut the tomatoes into wedges and the ham into fine strips. Arrange all the salad ingredients, including the olives, on four individual plates and serve with the mayonnaise. **Serves 4**

Mediterranean mixed salad

2 eggs
1 lettuce
6 tomatoes
2 green peppers
20 black olives
3 tablespoons olive oil
2 tablespoons cider vinegar
2 tablespoons apple juice
generous pinch each of salt, pepper and dried sage

Hard boil the eggs for 10 minutes, shell and cut them into wedges. Wash the lettuce and separate it into leaves, tearing larger ones in half. Leave it to drain. Cut the tomatoes into wedges. Halve the peppers, remove the seeds and pith and slice the flesh into strips. Mix the lettuce, tomatoes, green pepper and olives together in a large bowl.

Whisk the oil with the vinegar and apple juice. Season the dressing with salt, pepper and sage and pour it over the salad. Arrange the wedges of egg on top and serve. **Serves 4**

Sweet corn and tomato salad

6 tomatoes
1 small cucumber
$\frac{1}{2}$ (326-g/$11\frac{1}{2}$-oz) can sweet corn
1 small onion
2 tablespoons lemon juice
3 tablespoons oil
$\frac{1}{2}$ teaspoon salt
pinch each of pepper, sugar and garlic salt
2 tablespoons chopped fresh parsley or chives

Cut the tomatoes into quarters. Halve the cucumber lengthways and cut the halves into thin slices. Drain the sweet corn. Finely dice the onion.

Mix the lemon juice with the oil, diced onion, salt, pepper, sugar and garlic salt. Place the tomatoes in the centre of a salad plate, surround them with the sliced cucumber and arrange the sweet corn round the edge. Pour the dressing over the salad and sprinkle the chopped herbs on top.
Serves 4

Celery, carrot and apple salad

3 crisp dessert apples
squeeze of lemon
2 large carrots
4 sticks celery
1 tablespoon finely chopped walnut (optional)
1 tablespoon sultanas
4–6 tablespoons Mayonnaise (page 76)

Quarter, core and chop the apples, place them in a salad bowl and sprinkle them with lemon juice. Peel and grate the carrots. Trim and finely chop the celery. Add the chopped walnuts, if used. Mix the carrot, celery, walnuts and sultanas with the apple and stir in enough mayonnaise to coat all the ingredients.

Sweet corn and tomato salad.

Raw vegetable salad selection

(Illustrated opposite)

Radish salad
4 bunches of radishes
bunch of chives
salt and pepper

Carrot salad
4 large carrots
1 tablespoon lemon juice
1 tablespoon oil
2 teaspoons sugar
$\frac{1}{4}$ teaspoon salt
4 tablespoons lightly whipped cream

Red pepper and radish salad
1 red pepper
2 mouli (large white radishes) or 2 bunches
of ordinary radishes
1 teaspoon dried basil
salt

Pepper and onion salad
2 green peppers
1 red pepper
300 ml/$\frac{1}{2}$ pint hot water
2 onions
$\frac{1}{4}$ teaspoon paprika
salt and pepper

Cucumber and celeriac salad
1 cucumber
2 young celeriac
2 tablespoons lemon juice
$\frac{1}{2}$ red pepper
bunch of dill (optional)
pinch of sugar
salt and pepper

Red cabbage and apple salad
$\frac{1}{2}$ red cabbage
2 dessert apples
1 teaspoon sugar
salt and pepper

DRESSING
12 tablespoons oil
6 tablespoons wine vinegar

Trim and finely slice the radishes and arrange them in a salad bowl. Wash, drain and chop the chives and sprinkle them over the top, together with salt and pepper to taste.

Peel the carrots and grate them coarsely. Whisk together the lemon juice, oil, sugar and salt and stir the mixture into the carrot. Transfer the salad to a bowl and top it with the lightly whipped cream.

Cut the red pepper in half, remove the seeds and pith and slice the flesh into strips. Trim and coarsely grate the mouli or radishes and mix them in a bowl with the red pepper. Sprinkle the basil and salt to taste over the top.

Halve the green and red peppers, remove the seeds and pith and put them in a heatproof bowl. Pour over the hot water and leave the peppers to stand for a few minutes, then drain and dice them, together with the onions. Mix the pepper and onion together in a bowl and sprinkle the salad with the paprika and salt and pepper to taste.

Thinly slice the cucumber. Peel the celeriac and grate or cut it into fine strips. Sprinkle these with lemon juice and leave them on one side. Dice the red pepper, removing the seeds and pith. Wash, drain and chop the dill, if used. Mix the cucumber, celeriac, red pepper and dill in a salad bowl and sprinkle the salad with the sugar and salt and pepper to taste.

Remove the stalk and any outer damaged leaves from the red cabbage and cut it into strips. Plunge these into boiling water, cook for 5 minutes, then drain and leave to cool. Quarter and core the apples and cut them into pieces. Mix the cabbage and apple together in a bowl and sprinkle with the sugar and salt and pepper to taste.

Whisk together the oil and vinegar and pour a little dressing over each salad, with the exception of the carrot salad. **Serves 10-12**

Cauliflower salad

3 eggs
1 cauliflower
450 g/1 lb young carrots
bunch of parsley
5 tablespoons mayonnaise
3 tablespoons single cream
1–2 tablespoons lemon juice

Hard boil the eggs for 10 minutes, drain and allow them to cool. Shell and cut them into wedges. Wash the cauliflower, cut away the hard stalk and divide it into florets. Trim and wash the carrots and cut them into julienne strips. Bring two pans of salted water to the boil and blanch the cauliflower and carrot strips separately, giving the cauliflower 5 minutes and the carrots 2 minutes. Drain well and leave to cool.

Wash, drain and chop the parsley. Beat the mayonnaise with the cream and lemon juice to taste. Arrange the cauliflower and carrot in a salad bowl and mix in the dressing. Sprinkle the salad with parsley, garnish with the egg wedges and serve. **Serves 6**

Mixed pepper salad

(Illustrated on page 74)

4 green peppers
4 red peppers
2 onions
2 tablespoons olive oil
1 tablespoon vinegar
½ teaspoon salt
1 teaspoon freshly ground black pepper

Cut the peppers into rings, removing the stalks, seeds and pith. Slice the onions also into rings and mix them in a bowl with the green and red pepper. Whisk together the olive oil and vinegar, season the dressing with salt and pepper and pour it over the salad. **Serves 8**

Raw vegetable salad selection (page 72). *Clockwise from top left* Radish salad; Carrot salad; Red pepper and radish salad; Pepper and onion salad; Cucumber and celeriac salad; Red cabbage and apple salad.

Neapolitan salad

225 g/8 oz frozen peas
350 g/12 oz frozen French beans
225 g/8 oz carrots, cooked
3 eggs
2 (312-g/11-oz) cans artichoke hearts
30 stoned green olives
250 ml/8 fl oz Mayonnaise (page 76)
2 tablespoons chopped fresh parsley
3 tablespoons single cream
pinch each of paprika and sugar
1 teaspoon lemon juice
salt and pepper

Cook the frozen peas and beans in boiling salted water following the instructions on the packets, drain and leave to cool. Dice the carrots. Hard boil the eggs for 10 minutes, plunge them into cold water and shell them. Dice two eggs and cut the third into wedges. Drain the artichoke hearts and cut them into pieces. Slice the olives into rings. Combine the peas, beans, chopped carrot, diced egg, artichoke and olives in a large bowl.

Mix the mayonnaise with the chopped parsley, cream, paprika, sugar, lemon juice and salt and pepper to taste and fold the dressing into the salad ingredients. Garnish the salad with the egg wedges and serve. **Serves 6–8**

Potato and pepper salad

1.5 kg/3 lb potatoes (preferably new)
4 onions
5 pickled cucumbers
3 red peppers
4 tablespoons wine vinegar
8 tablespoons oil
½ teaspoon salt
¼ teaspoon white pepper
8 tablespoons chopped fresh mixed herbs

Wash the potatoes well, place them in a pan containing boiling water, cover and simmer for 20 minutes. Drain and leave to cool.

Dice the onions. Drain and dice the pickled cucumbers. Halve the red peppers, remove the seeds and pith and dice the flesh. Peel and thinly slice the potatoes. Mix the potato, onion, cucumber and pepper together in a bowl. Whisk the vinegar with the oil, salt, pepper and herbs and pour the dressing over the salad. Cover the bowl and leave to stand at room temperature.
Serves 6–8

Bean and sweet corn salad

1 (424-g/15-oz) can kidney beans
1 (425-g/15-oz) can sweet corn
2 onions
2 tablespoons wine vinegar
4 tablespoons oil
½ teaspoon salt
¼ teaspoon white pepper
2 teaspoons crushed fresh or 1 teaspoon dried rosemary
sprig of fresh rosemary to garnish (optional)

Drain the beans and sweet corn. Finely dice the onions. Mix the beans, sweet corn and onion together in a bowl.

Make a dressing with the vinegar, oil, salt, pepper and rosemary and stir it into the salad. Garnish with a sprig of rosemary, if liked. **Serves 6**

Top, from the left Neapolitan salad; Potato and pepper salad.
Bottom Bean and sweet corn salad; Mixed pepper salad (page 73).

Creamy cucumber salad

1 large or 2 small cucumbers
1 small lettuce
bunch of dill or mint
1 (142-ml/5-fl oz) carton single or double cream
pinch of mustard powder
2 tablespoons natural yogurt
pinch of sugar
generous pinch of pepper
$\frac{1}{2}$–1 teaspoon salt·

Peel the cucumber, if the skin is tough, and grate or slice it very finely. Wash the lettuce, separate the leaves and drain them thoroughly. Wash, drain and chop the dill or mint.

Beat the cream with the mustard, yogurt, sugar, pepper and salt to taste and stir in the chopped herbs. Line a salad bowl with lettuce leaves and fill the centre with the cucumber salad. Spoon the dressing on top. **Serves 4–6**

Creamy cucumber salad.

Horseradish cream

1 (142-ml/5-fl oz) carton double cream
$\frac{1}{4}$ teaspoon salt
pinch each of white pepper and sugar
1 tablespoon grated fresh horseradish
or 1–2 tablespoons bottled horseradish

Whip the cream until stiff and stir in the salt, pepper, sugar and horseradish. If you are using bottled horseradish you may need to add a little more than with fresh, as the bottled variety never tastes as strong. **Serves 4**

Serve with: Spit-roast or grilled beef and hamburgers.

Mayonnaise

2 egg yolks
generous pinch each of salt, pepper and mustard powder
300 ml/$\frac{1}{2}$ pint oil
1$\frac{1}{2}$ tablespoons wine vinegar
1$\frac{1}{2}$ tablespoons warm water

Beat the egg yolks with the salt, pepper and mustard. Gradually beat in the oil, drop by drop, until the mixture thickens, then stir in a little vinegar. Continue adding the oil until it is all absorbed, beating in a little more vinegar every time the mayonnaise becomes thick. Gently stir in any remaining vinegar with the water and serve. **Serves 8**

NOTE Always remember to add the oil as carefully as possible as if it is poured in too quickly the mayonnaise will curdle. You can still save it, however, by beating another egg yolk in a separate bowl and gradually adding the curdled mixture, drop by drop, as before.

Sauce vinaigrette

2 small onions
1 large gherkin (optional)
1–2 tablespoons wine vinegar
2 teaspoons Dijon mustard
5 tablespoons oil
generous pinch each of sugar and freshly ground
pepper
½ teaspoon salt
8 tablespoons chopped fresh mixed herbs
(parsley, chives, basil, marjoram, tarragon)

Finely dice the onions. Drain and dice the gherkin, if used. Whisk together the vinegar, mustard, oil, sugar, pepper and salt and stir in the chopped herbs and vegetables. Transfer the mixture to a sauceboat and leave it to stand for a while before serving. **Serves 4**

Serve with: All kinds of green and vegetable salads and freshly cooked vegetables such as French beans.

Creamy mustard sauce

about 4 tablespoons single cream
150 ml/¼ pint Mayonnaise (page 76)
1–2 tablespoons mild wholegrain or Dijon
mustard
pinch of sugar
dash of lemon juice (optional)
1 lettuce heart to garnish (optional)

Stir enough cream into the mayonnaise to give a pouring consistency, then mix in the mustard to taste. Add the sugar and lemon juice, if liked. Cut the lettuce heart into quarters, if used. Transfer the sauce to a bowl and garnish it with the lettuce quarters. **Serves 4**

Serve with: Barbecued steaks, hamburgers, kebabs and other meats, sausage dishes and salads.

Avocado sauce

3 ripe avocados
4 tablespoons natural yogurt
1 tablespoon lemon juice or to taste
½ teaspoon salt
½ teaspoon white pepper
1 teaspoon fresh or ½ teaspoon dried tarragon

Halve the avocados, remove the stones and scoop out the flesh. Place this in a bowl and mash it to a thick cream with a fork. Mix in the yogurt, lemon juice, salt, pepper and tarragon and chill the sauce in the refrigerator. **Serves 4–6**

Serve with: Grilled poultry, veal and raw vegetable salads.

Herb and cream cheese sauce

1 dessert apple
175 g/6 oz cream cheese
1 tablespoon sugar
3 tablespoons dry white wine
1 tablespoon lemon juice
1 teaspoon fresh or bottled grated horseradish
1 (142-ml/5-fl oz) carton whipping cream
¼ teaspoon paprika
4 tablespoons chopped fresh mixed herbs
(parsley, chives, tarragon)

Peel and grate the apple. Mash the cream cheese with a fork and mix in the grated apple, sugar, white wine, lemon juice and horseradish to give a smooth sauce. Whip the cream until stiff and fold it into the cheese mixture, followed by the paprika and chopped herbs. Transfer to a sauceboat or bowl and serve. **Serves 4–6**

Serve with: Mildly flavoured meat, fish or poultry.

Index